SCRIPT FOR A SYNTHETIC PLAY

On (Un)grounding community
and the generative power of fiction

ONO
MATO
PEE
172

COLLECTED TEXTS

WELCOME TO UNKNOWN GROUNDS

by Flora Reznik,
artistic director of Unknown Grounds

Ground, foundation, reason, land, landscape, territory, earth, soil, dirt, dust. Synonyms bring nuances and changes of perspectives on the same or the similar.

Ground is background. It is onto the landscape that all images appear. There is no form of the self that is dissociated from that background: it informs identity. Territory is our link to others, and therefore is what makes us vulnerable. It is what shakes our certainties, something that we cannot completely grasp. We exist within it, but need to make sense out of it, using the most refined technology as well as our own complex and malleable perception system. Territory is a construct formed by myth, stories, facts, memory, fiction, and pure will. Territory allows for a sense of rootedness, but also dispossession and resistance.

Who will be the actors of future social transformations and how will their identity and engagements influence the nature of these transformations? What happens when ideas hit the ground? Where do we stand when we use the term "we"? The recursive nature of this question sets us on course to complicate the notion and practice of 'the commons', understood as the values and resources we need to share because of physical proximity within a territory. The commons set out for collective performance, to be negotiated and constantly re-defined. The self, the community and the environment form an unstable triangle. How then to deal with this co-constituency? What strategies of belonging for temporary, fragile, and singular communities can emerge
from this point of departure?

Today, the need to invest effort into rethinking community is strikingly urgent: anti-intellectualism and polarisation are on the rise around the globe, and it is no coincidence that democracy is being questioned with increasing openness as powerful societies choose to push their limits in the direction of a form of politics that should be clearly called fascism. Simultaneously, some democratic agendas push discourses on behalf of the "common good" or the "public interest" as if these were pre-existing, indisputable entities, promoting cultural merchandise as "accessible to all". This gesture of unification and simplification should alarm us as well. "Social and economic questions are oversimplified, and the potentially critical originality of the concerned gesture is abandoned and surrendered to normalization and domestication."[1] In light of this reality, we should eagerly refuse to simplify. A pluralistic community will have to deal with internal tensions that undermine the certainty of a ‚common ground'.

The proposal of this book is to consider that we don't sufficiently know the grounds on which we stand, since such grounds are always contested territory, defined in a mix of languages, some of which we don't master. Taking this as a point of departure, we ask: do we want to stand, or do we want to move? Can we oscillate between these two practices? Between knowledge and uncertainty? Can we have a conversation on the move? Can that conversation be creative and playful? Unsurprisingly, these questions challenge our usual means of communication, which brings us to consider the realm of the senses, affects and performativity. New strategies need to be created in order to deal with a vast range of urgent topics. We need tools for radical non isolation[2]. For example, it is a challenging task to read texts from an alien field, but if we read together, we might be able to step onto uncharted territories. By borrowing tools from the performance arts, we may tackle the plasticity that we bare inside and that takes different configurations in each encounter, enabling a synthetic and playful sense of self and of community towards a new understanding of living dynamics of togetherness and relating.

What's unknown can seem strange and awkward. We shall welcome the perspective of the stranger, the newcomer and outsider who doesn't speak the language correctly, as we shall recognize the stranger in ourselves. We must practice strange ways of dealing with questions, strange ways of conversating, and even stranger ways of behaving and sensing our environment. Instead of levelling the ground, we aim for deep plunges and high climbs, facing the difficulty presented by uneven terrains. The crossroads of established disciplines and personal experiences are unstable surfaces propitious for adventurous gatherings at the edges of everyone's comfort zones.

For us, the catalyst for innovation is hybridization[3]: letting an identity be contaminated with something else. This doesn't automatically make innovative discourse good or useful, but risks must be taken, since old tools cannot address the complexity of an ever-changing reality. We stand on unknown grounds. We are called to put our minds and our bodies to work, but it is crucial to work collectively with others. When we work collectively, the chance to incorporate new tools into our practices is far greater. It is both an epistemological affirmation and a political one. The notion of foundation or ground is conceptual, imaginary, but not any less real, even if we don't all agree on its meaning or cannot grasp its effects. We need a collective speculative reflection about the link between these two spheres of reality we occupy: the conceptual *and* the concrete. The conceptual realm is the potentiality of the here and now. To think other worlds might seem impossible, but we can think our world otherwise and, in this way, find unexplored potentials in it.

The fictional treatment in this book is triggered by the conviction that fiction can enrich our appreciation of, and agency in, reality. This is the generative power of fiction. The idea to bring the conversation into the form of a script is inspired by „The frogs" by Aristophanes because we value the public and accessible aspects of Ancient Greek Comedy and poetry as a vehicle to bring complex political issues to people's minds. Frogs are hybrid beings capable of living under, on and above the ground (when they jump). Changing perspective in relation to ground is always useful. Aristophanes' frogs speak an animal language, prompting the human characters to react in unusual ways. This book's chorus sometimes behaves like frogs, bringing questions and opinions born from their personal experiences in a language foreign to the expertise of the curated authors. Thus, experience and expertise mingle to produce a hybrid language that is surprising, inviting and promising.

This book is an effort to produce an experimental archiving of the ephemeral experiences and discussions among special guests and a group of participants, which took place during 21 & 22 November 2019 during the performative symposium Unknown Grounds. The first part, ‚Script for a Synthetic Play', is a fictionalized text by Nathaniel Feldmann based on the transcripts of those conversations, stylized for dramatic effect into the form of a script of a theater play. They were prompted by a collection of texts curated for the occasion and written by the guests: seven short texts to be found on the second part of the book titled „Collected texts", about human and land exhaustion, new world making technologies, the need for refuge and infrastructures of care, cultural and deep time changes, among other topics. A set of questions sent by the participants prior to the event about those texts read in solitude is also included. Later on, those questions, together with the texts, were used as entry points for a collective experience framed in a theatrical atmosphere where the generative power of fiction unfolded.

Taking this strange order of events into account, a question arises: Does a script based on fragments of transcribed conversations taken out of their original context refer to a past, present or future? Throughout the script, the Ancient Greek Comedy elements become contaminated by a pinch of Science Fiction, as the text functions as a time-space bending dispositive of sorts. The script points to a future performance (as a script always does), while its content is based on a past event. The conversations that led up to the 'Script for a Synthetic Play' exist in documentation and in the memory of those who attended. Memory often confuses moments, condenses meanings, confronts issues that went unnoticed, imagines alternative trajectories. By allowing ourselves to modify the order in which things took place during the event, we emphasize conflict and the clashing of ideas, which in some cases remained tacit in the actual conversations due to, we suspect, social decorum. The fictional strategy proved to help highlight fruitful crossroads. In remembering, we also emphasize agency and the processual aspect of collective thinking and discussions as sites of production of knowledge.

"Synthetic", according to one definition, is a product made from artificial substances. But if a whole discussion revolves around the very notion of what is natural, can we rest assured that we know what we are saying when we say something is artificial in this sense? Perhaps a better definition, one that inspired the title of this piece of writing, is that something synthetic concerns form more than content. It is something put together artificially, artfully, hopefully even playfully?

The first scene of the script features an alien voice addressing the performers from an unidentified location, urging them to figure out how to move on an uneven and unknown terrain, as they encounter „sitting devices“ (it‘s all a silly joke, of course they are chairs, but the idea is to denaturalize experience, and it works! If you want to believe, and you are willing to engage with what‘s at stake) and each other. Some of the members of the chorus start speaking in strange languages, as they approach a glowing red box that conceals a treasure, which turns out to be a myriad of questions.

The cast of this script resembles the people present at the event in Leeuwarden: our guests take the leading roles, and are asked to perform unexpected tasks, placed into awkward positions, and made to encounter hardly plausible situations. It is based on actual events, but it is not an actual transcript of the event. As a counterpoint, the 25 participants, who in real life have names, rich personalities, and fascinating occupations, take the role of a chorus in the fashion of a Greek comedy, constituting a collective voice that carries the dramatic flow, that from time to time manages to disintegrate and add a pinch of anachronistic individuality to the performance through their singular voices.

Another observation about the notion of synthesis. By making fictional use of the figure of the chorus, we by no means aimed to present the voices of the performers as a coherent whole, or to form a definitive solution where individualities dissolved once and for all. On the contrary, it‘s important to remember that there lay voices in tension, in relation without resolution. Only this tension can be generative.

Finally, ‚synthetic‘ stands for artificial, for a stance on the side of the generative power of fiction, against crystallized historical constructions that are taken for immovable reality, naturalized. Once we discard that anything is natural (in the sense we have just indicated), and instead see every aspect of our surroundings and even of ourselves as social constructs that have sedimented over time, we realize our world is made of fictions, which are strong and effective as long as they are not contested. Only then can we start to critically address the structures that have become historically solidified, and to playfully imagine new ones. In the context of this publication, through fictionalizing these documented traces of conversations that took place during the event, we were able to speculate and make bold propositions.

The idea behind the structure of this book is that by the time the reader gets to the texts that prompted these conversations, they encounter them as if they were written by friends, or characters they know. The texts are not meant to be secluded works, but provocations inviting us to intervene. Texts that function as props[4] as long as they are put into play. In turn, a script is a tool with cues for enacting, that encourages open imagination and multiple actualizations. The play is an invitation to become fragmented and multiple, in tight relation to others.

Inspired by the process of conceiving this project, we dare say that our reality may be a mesh of intertwined fictions with many loose threads and surprising plot twists. We can't escape the linearity of the written word, but we hope the reader feels free to engage with the text as if entering unknown grounds: let the generative power of fiction undermine established certainties about how to read, indulging in a meandering and perhaps disorienting experience through the text.

1 Rebekka Kiesewetter, in “The Relay Conversations. Post-digital publishing”, a publication project by art initiative The Reading Room, online publication, 2018, https://instrumentinventors.org/research/relay conversation the reading room 27 28 post digital publishing/

2 The notion of ‚radical non isolation‘ is borrowed from one of the authors in this book, Theun Karelse.

3 Razmig Keucheyan, The Left Hemisphere. Mapping Criti cal Theory Today, translated by Gregory Elliot, Verso, 2014, p.62

4 Fred Moten and Stefano Harney, The Undercommons: Fugitive Planning and Black Study, MLA, 2013, Chapter 7 „The General Antagonism, an interview with Stevphen Shukaitis“: „(...) there are these props, these toys, and if you pick them up you can move into some new thinking and into a new set of relations, a new way of being together, thinking together. In the end, it’s the new way of being together and thinking together that’s important, and not the tool, not the prop. Or, the prop is important only insofar as it allows you to enter; but once you’re there, it’s the relation and the activity that’s really what you want to emphasize.“, p. 106.

SCRIPT FOR A SYNTHETIC PLAY

"'Brekekeks koaks koaks'
I learned this from you."
Aristophanes, Frogs 250–251

Cast

(In order of appearance)

Chorus

Moderator

Contributors
masharu
Ribal El-Khatib[1]
Bert Looper
Andrej Radman
Flora Reznik
Theun Karelse
Sissel Tonn

1

PROLOGUE

ON THE NOTION OF ORIGIN

Leeuwarden, Friesland
Tresoar – Frysk Histoarysk en Letterkundich Sintrum

The members of the Chorus are ushered through to the side of the stage, down a set of stairs, and into a blacked-out space in the form of a circle in front of an elevated stage. The tribune remains empty. Ethereal music plays from all angles. An alien-like, yet soothing voice enters from numerous points of the room, travelling around the stage, hovering over everyone's confused heads:

"Hello stranger, welcome to unknown grounds. Please be aware of the uneven terrain, and others within your proximity. Move with caution. Explore your surroundings, but do not enter the circle. As your eyes adjust to the darkness, indulge your curiosity.

Please approach the circle. If you have a flashlight, turn it off and set it on the floor. Place your hands on top of the dotted edge. (Pause. The speaker is observing when each of the participants have done this). Good. Once you have a firm grip of a solid object, drag the object while taking a step backwards. This breaks the circle.
What is this object? You may or may not have guessed... it is a sitting device.

Now listen carefully, be precise: let go of the sitting device and move one step to your left. Yes, that's good. Listen even closer now: move two steps forward. Then take one step to your right.

In whatever manner that suits you, you can now take a seat on the sitting device."

Like lightning, bright, colourful, state-of-the-art lights flash at the centre of the circle: red, green, blue. Seven bodies that should have been on the stage appear out of nothingness in the middle of the dirt floor circle and are suddenly illuminated. They circulate through a cloud of smoke that travels around the room, which produces the illusion that they are not walking, but floating. They turn their backs to the chorus, and encircle a small, wooden box. They seem to be navigating what to do with it, but their voices aren't clear. Eventually one of the group picks it up and turns to the chorus. She starts speaking in a language that nobody can understand. She passes the box to someone else, who in turn begins to speak in another language, incomprehensible to the audience, as if this box had the power to make people speak in tongues. Yet everyone listens carefully.[1]

1 For translations in English, go to Appendix.

FLORA

Hola, soy Flora Reznik. Estoy muy entusiasmada por hablar con todos ustedes. Vengo de Argentina, donde hablamos un Español a la italiana. Se van a dar cuenta que siempre muevo mis manos cuando hablo. Soy artista y junto con un grupo de gente increíble organizamos este evento para preguntarnos qué es... hmm... la palabra en Castellano no me sirve. Bueno, ya hablaremos después.

MASHARU

Меня зовут Маша, я любитель земли. Я хочу поделиться с вами практикой поедания земли, и вам решать, пробовать или нет.

RIBAL

مرحباً بالجميع، اسمي ريبال، مساعد مهندس معماري وأنا طالب لجوء في هولندا، لذا فأنا أعيش هنا مؤقتاً وآمل أن أتمكن من البقاء.

أنا من المجهول! حرفيا من المجهول !! سأترك الباقي لفقرتي غدا وسأتحدث عنه أكثر، نراكم غدا

ANDREJ

Ja sam Andrej Radman, hrvatski arhitekt koji predaje teoriju u Nizozemskoj. Dugo sam se pretstavljao kao arhitekt zainteresiran za teoriju. Odnedavno sam zaključio kako to vise nije slucaj. Praksa nije suprotna teoriji. Ono što je primarno jest djelovanje, prakticno i teoretsko. Pace, djelovanje na djelovanje, prije nego li dosegnemo opipljivu razinu.
Veselim se zajedno s Vama promisljati pojam uzemljenja.

THEUN

Ik bin Theun Karelse uut Borssele, dat is un klein durpje in Zeeland, bie de kerncentrale. Bie oas wor dialect hesproke, me da kan best noga flienk verschille. Oas praote in ZuudBeveland bevorbeeld glad oars dan in Zeeuw Vlaanderen, watta tegenover mekare ligt an de Westerschelde.

BERT

Hoi, wolkom elkenien yn Tresoar, Schatkamer fan Fryslân, dat is it bewarplak fan 'e skiednis fan Fryslân. Ik bin Bert Looper, direkteur fan dizze ynstelling, en histoarikus fan berop. ik bin tige bliid om ûnder jimme allegearre te wêzen, en ik bin bliid om it begryp fan iepen mienskip te besprekken.

SISSEL

Hej mit navn er Sissel, Jeg er en dansk kunstner der bor her i Holland — i Haag. I mit kunstneriske arbejde er jeg interesseret i hvordan vi opfatter, sanser og reagerer på de (menneskeskabte) forandringer, vi oplever i vores omgivelser. Jeg tager ofte udgangspunkt i en stedspecifik situation, hvor mennesker oplever miljømæssige forandringer, og zoomer ind på de ting, der er mindre håndgribelige, såsom sanselige oplevelser, der svæver på tærsklen af, hvad vi kan fornemme og forstå.

As if the sun were rising, the room is warmed with soft light from the edges and along the walls of the circular pit where everyone stands. The circle of listeners situated closer to the edges emerge from the fog and become visible. Those who just spoke leave the centre and climb a set of steps that lead them directly to the stage.

CHORUS

I'm a teacher.
I'm very uncomfortable with professional titles.
I am a writer.

I don't know what I am.
I'm an architect. I'm a filmmaker.
I'm a dancer and theatre maker.
I'm working as an artist.
I am an artist and researcher.
I will say that I'm a public space or landscape artist.
I'm trained as an art historian.
I'm an artist.
I am working as a conceptual artist.
I'm a master's student.

MODERATOR

standing on an elevated spot in the rear of the circle

Where are you all coming from?

CHORUS

I'm from Amsterdam.
I come from Germany.
I'm from Utrecht.
I've been very nomadic.
I'm from Russia.
I live in Den Haag, but I come from Denmark.
I'm originally from Leeuwarden.
I have lived in France.
I was born and raised in Greece.
I come from Argentina.
I am originally from Croatia.
I don't belong anywhere, and I don't know anything.
My home is in Rotterdam.
I live in Groningen.
I come from a very nice night's sleep last night.

With an agile jump, one of the circle members, masharu gets down from the stage and whilst walking freely around the entire space where the chorus is, speaks.

MASHARU

I don't know exactly where my roots are. I am very confused, I think. Even as I live in the Netherlands, I will always be an immigrant, even now after I have been granted a Dutch passport.

masharu returns to the stage and a few moments pass before the next contributor addresses the crowd, as if waiting to gain the courage to take the leap forward. Ribal looks out across the circle of faces.

RIBAL

taking a deep breath

I'm literally from the unknown.

CHORUS

How is that possible? You must be from somewhere?

RIBAL

It's difficult to have a clear answer. I'm an asylum seeker. This is the reason why I came to the Netherlands. I don't have a passport. I am listed as Staatloze, or stateless.

I was born in Abu Dhabi, and I lived there for thirty-five years, but I'm not a citizen of the Arab Emirates. I don't belong there. I have a traveling document and it's handwritten. Recently, I received my papers from Lebanon. It's very confusing, because the document is Lebanese, but inside it says I'm Palestinian.

CHORUS, ONE

But where are you from, please tell us!

CHORUS, TWO

Are you Palestinian or are you Lebanese?

RIBAL

clearing his throat

Are you asking where I come from or what I am? How can those two questions become mixed so often? I was born in one country, but I have a travel document from another country. And that document says that I'm from a third country by nationality, and I'm now living in a fourth country, and still not a citizen of any of them.

I can't say exactly where I'm from. I'm waiting for my papers to be able to prove that. This is my struggle.

The light intensifies on Ribal's face.

CHORUS, THREE

to Ribal

Could you become an E-citizen of Estonia?

RIBAL

laughing

And where would I live? In a USB flash stick?

Ribal steps back and the lights fade above the contributors. The spotlight meanders for a while as if hesitating, and finally drops on the moderator, as if it didn't know where else to land.

MODERATOR

speaking in a matter-of-fact manner

Thanks everyone for introducing yourselves. As you all know by now, this is not a traditional symposium. We want this to be a collective effort of shared responsibilities. The main role of Unknown Grounds is not to fully comprehend what we will encounter, but to explore the complexities and experience them together. The unknown is an opportunity for us to learn.

The spotlight goes off and the space returns to darkness. A drum-roll begins from each corner and ends in a crash of a gong!

MODERATOR

Let's begin.

2

LANDSCAPE AND LANGUAGE

(UN)GROUNDING "GROUND"

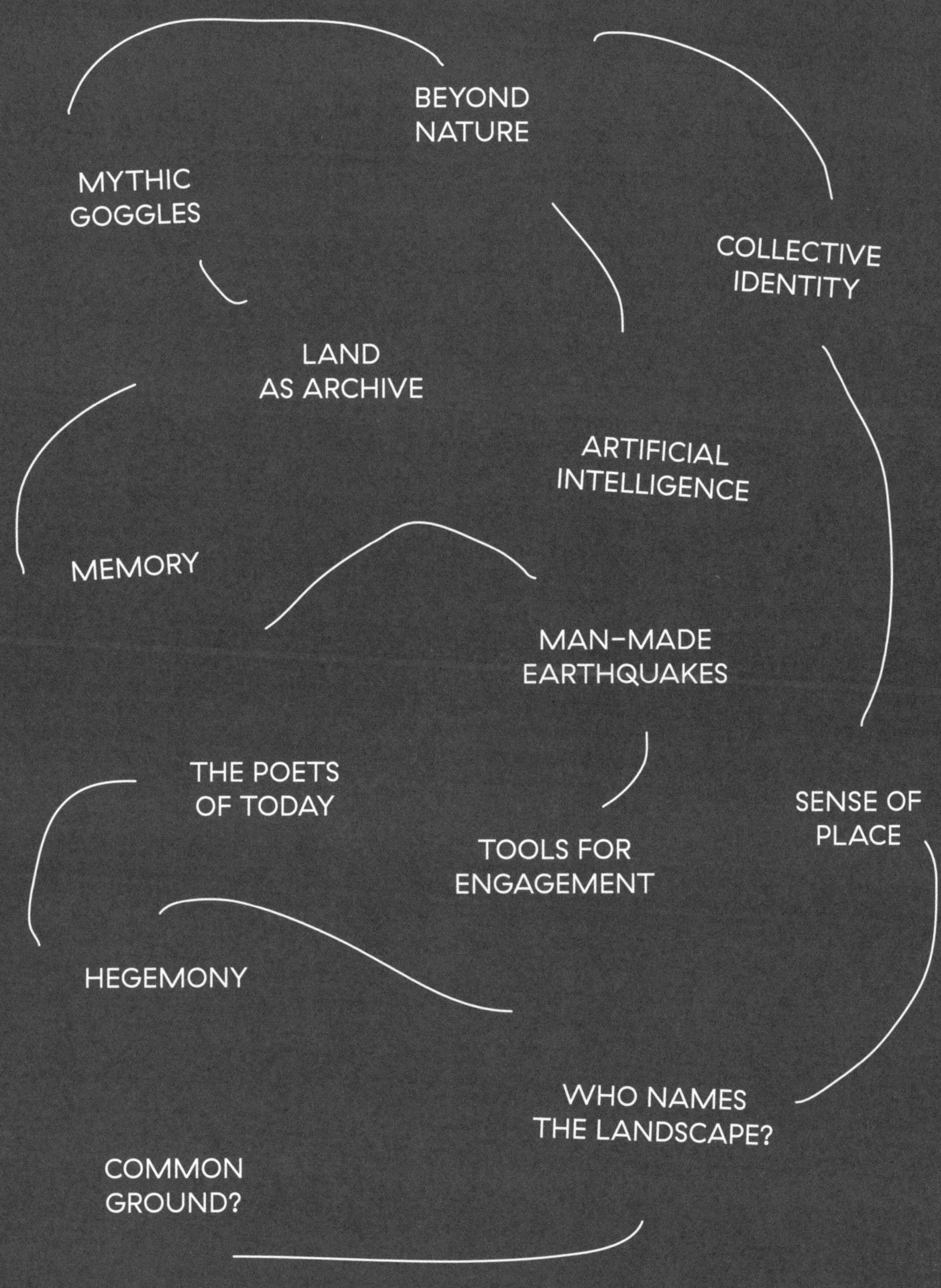
BEYOND
NATURE
MYTHIC
GOGGLES
COLLECTIVE
IDENTITY
LAND
AS ARCHIVE
ARTIFICIAL
INTELLIGENCE
MEMORY
MAN-MADE
EARTHQUAKES
THE POETS
OF TODAY
SENSE OF
PLACE
TOOLS FOR
ENGAGEMENT
HEGEMONY
WHO NAMES
THE LANDSCAPE?
COMMON
GROUND?

The lights gradually brighten from the edges of the space, like the sky before dawn. The chorus takes their place in the pit. The contributors sit at the edge of the stage. They look at one another, forming a circle. A member of the chorus is eagerly waiting to address the contributors and raises their hand with shaking enthusiasm.

CHORUS, ONE

to everyone

What do we mean when we say landscape?

Theun smiles with a cheeky grin, eager to take part in the play. He moves slightly forward, swinging his feet and softly kicking with his heel.

THEUN

In the Middle Ages we had what was called a 'Landscape of Symbols', you can see that Medieval paintings represent the landscape insofar as it communicates a symbolic meaning: landscape as the background of human endeavours. By the Renaissance this changed to a Landscapes of Fact[1]: observation and the representation of what is in front of the human gaze became relevant.

But what is this fact? What if the field where we are is unknown grounds? Where are we walking through? Do we know? I've been reading a lot of books and walking through a lot of landscapes, and I thought I knew Europe and I thought I knew the Dutch landscape and yet the more I read, the less I think I know about it. Do we know the field? Is it this sort of massive erosion that we have placed upon biodiversity?

From a 'landscape of symbols' in the Middle Age to a 'landscape of fact' during the Renaissance, what are we now?

1 Landscapes of Symbols and Landscapes of Fact: See Theun Karelse, *Machine Wilderness* – Paragraphs 1 and 2.

A silence fills the stage, as if everyone had forgotten there was ever a script. Eventually, a member of the chorus, avoiding answering, proposes a new question.

CHORUS, TWO

Shall we set off into a historical conversation about where the word landscape comes from? Originally the word meant something like a manageable area, a unit that can be measured. In Dutch there's the word *Landschap*, so it's about an area that is governed by, or managed by, people.

BERT

If we talk about a cultural landscape, we might ask: how do we make our ground part of our individual and collective identity using words? It is about power. The power of language to shape our sense of place[2]. Of course, there is always a triangular relationship: it's not only about language and landscape, but it is essentially about language, landscape, *and* memory[3]. While language is frozen in memory in many aspects, how does language, how do the words we use, relate to the rapidly changing environment? Are we able to name everything around us in the 21st century state? Or is there a growing discrepancy between

2 Sense of place: See Bert Looper, *Unknown words, unknown grounds. Language, landscape, and memory,* Paragraphs 5 and 6, 11 and 12.

3 Language, landscape and memory: See Bert Looper, *Unknown words, unknown grounds. Language, landscape, and memory,* Paragraphs 1 to 3, 11 and 12.

reality and language? Is language betraying us? Is language a barrier from seeing what is going on? Is language more and more a result of consolation or is it leading us towards actions?

CHORUS, THREE

I once did a project on a field of four-square kilometres, and I would tell people: 'This is your food. Go into it and eat'. We chose a pretty random piece of this area, and there was no food, or there was almost none, a couple of flowers, a couple of roots, and the rest was corn that first had to be digested by the cows before it became milk, etc. To gain access to the land, to enter this four-square kilometre patch, we needed the permission of the owners, but the owner didn't use the land, they just rented it out. There was no rental document where you can find out who was renting that land. This made me think that we are losing the landscape, in a very fundamental way, it's no longer of any importance if a poet writes correctly about a city and incorrectly about a rural area, either way, we've lost it.

Poets cannot describe the landscape anymore, simply *because* there is no engagement with the landscape anymore. So how can we work intimately with it? It seems that we are not dependent on it anymore, so the engagement is gone. I think then we might want to ask instead about the power of language. Do we need it? Yes. Because that power is part of our memory. Our memory is fixed in language, and words can live longer than a story. But if you miss the story behind it, then words can lose their meaning too.

THEUN

Maybe today Artificial Intelligence is naming the landscape. But what are they learning from? Aren't they reproducing human biases, even our ignorance?[4] I would say that with these new minds, these new ones that aren't visual, they very much mirror our dictionaries, they mirror how little, or how low a priority we have given to some animals and plants. That's what I want to mention with AI, it is just so geared towards people that it's problematic. Why should something be considered intelligent only if it is like a human? That is also part of the same question.

4 AI: See Theun Karelse, *Machine Wilderness*, Paragraph 4 and 5.

A member of the Chorus approaches the microphone, clearing their throat.

CHORUS

to Theun

Do you want AI to rule the world?

THEUN

I am not saying that machines will solve anything. What I'm saying is that our landscapes are full of machines. I'm interested in machines[5], not so much machines in and of themselves, but in how they can expose our mindset as their creators.

5 Machines: See Theun Karelse, *Machine Wilderness*, Paragraphs 3 to 6.

I'm not saying machines shouldn't be part of our landscape either. What I *care* about is the regeneration of landscapes. Imagine that there is an Artificial

Intelligence who is in charge of this landscape, who is a custodian for this island. What would its information source be, where would it get its information from? And where would it be able to act, how could it act?

Bert dusts off his jacket and calmly, stands up to speak, an idea for discussion on his mind.

BERT

As we have enhanced our power to determine nature, we have also rendered it less able to converse with us. We find it hard to imagine nature outside the use/value framework. We've become experts for analysing what nature can do for us but lack the language to consider what it can do *to* us. The former is important, the latter is vital.

Martin Heidegger identified a version of this trend in 1954, he observed that with the rise of technology, the technological imagination had converted the whole universe of beings into, what he called, an undifferentiated standing reserve, available for any use that humans decide. The rise of the standing reserve as a concept has bequeathed an inadequate and unsatisfying relationship with the natural world and therefore with us too.

Theun takes the microphone into his hand, waiting for Bert to return to his place amongst the other contributors.

THEUN

Exactly, but my work tries to challenge the convention of perceiving machines as assets of the human domain (in the sense that the biosphere and technosphere do not exist as separate realms). It is more about the understanding that machines are part of our landscape. Which currently translates as mining, self-driving cars, industrial agriculture. We pointed the Google AI platform at a section of the landscape to analyse images and asked it to tell us what it saw. When we showed it the view from the kitchen window in Finland, just a forest covered in snow, it said "snowmobiles."

Somehow these machines seem to grow up in an area where they can name a snowmobile, but not a tree, or snow. So, we thought we needed to question who or where these machines are learning from.

The members of the Chorus move to their designated spots, it seems that something is pushing from the inside, threatening to dismember the circle. A member of the Chorus suddenly jumps out of the circle and takes a microphone, with a troubled look in their eyes.

CHORUS

You mean 'us'?

THEUN

I think for our contemporary Western culture, the biggest issues we are facing exist in open spaces, which 'we' are only a small part of. I'm interested in engaging in how we, as humans, as well as other organic beings and in-organic beings acquire environmental literacy.

Another member of the Chorus enters the light, raising their hand to speak, but seems to have forgotten their question and instead returns to their place. Another member who has been looking at the ground for a while, as if concerned with other issues, takes a pinch of dirt in their hands and ceremoniously lets it slip through their fingers. Once they have gotten everyone's attention, they speak.

CHORUS

How does a landscape keep memory? How does it store it? And can we access it?

BERT

the spotlight shines down onto him

If you dig in the soil, you can find roots and learn what plants grew there. It's possible that there is memory, an archive in the soil, because you can go back in time, dig deep, and find something. We can see what has happened and use this information to go forward. It's not that we keep going back, it's that we need to maintain access to our memory, because being without memory is like living with dementia, people cannot make decisions, people cannot remember. Memory is vital.

CHORUS, ONE

I met a person who worked with dementia patients, and she said she would take them back to the landscape of their birth, back to the house of their birth and it would restore a lot of their memories. But everything had changed. She also said that this rapid urban renewal that we live in, of tearing everything down and building new is a collective loss of memory and identity. It's not unique to the rural landscape, it's happening everywhere.

Another member of the chorus leaves the crowd to speak for themselves after first politely raising their hand.

CHORUS, TWO

I think that landscape is the result of the interaction between man and nature and as such, it is a living archive, it is ever changing, it has no boundaries. It's undefined. Thus, we can't fully know it.

Sissel raises her hand to speak, asking for permission from the stage. Her eyes sparkle in the spotlight as she steps down and into the centre of the pit, engaging everyone's attention around her, ready to address the Chorus.

SISSEL

But you can learn a lot from digging into the soil. I learnt about the landscape surrounding Groningen[6] and its province from digging, and how in the 1960s

6 Groningen Gas Field: See Sissel Marie Tonn, Daily Research, Paragraphs 24 and 25.

the largest gas field in Northern Europe was discovered. Since then, gas has been extracted from this field and later people started feeling earthquakes and started raising concerns about it. Yet it wasn't until the mid-90s that the government acknowledged that these earthquakes were a result of the gas industry.

The subsurface of this country is extremely well surveyed. It is one of the most well surveyed sub-surfaces in the world. At almost every five-kilometre interval there has been a core sample[7] taken to try and understand what is going on below the surface. But still these earthquakes are very unpredictable. You cannot plan exactly what will happen when you start extracting materials that have existed in the same place in the earth for millions of years, materials that have been sitting in sediment for so long. We have suddenly created technologies that can pull gas from the ground and create a completely new relationship to how we interact with the earth. The same technologies leave behind huge voids in the ground that can cause collapse and shift without notice.

7 Core Samples: See Sissel Marie Tonn, Daily Research, everywhere in her text.

What I was most fascinated by was this term 'Man-Made Earthquakes'[8]. It's a phenomenon that is happening in the North of the Netherlands. For me it is a strange term because 'earthquake' reminds me of a force of nature, nature ravaging us in a way that there is nothing we can do.

8 Man-made earthquakes: See Sissel Marie Tonn, Daily Research, Paragraph 5 to 7.

I had the chance to travel to Groningen and stay with some people that I had met online who showed me around the area and who had a very different way of describing this 'Man-Made Earthquake' phenomenon I had been researching. They had very precise descriptions of the sensation of these man-made earthquakes. Some could feel the earthquakes before they happened.

A member of the Chorus takes hold of the microphone, they have energy in their step, standing by Sissel's side.

CHORUS

I live in Groningen. I've experienced these Man-Made Earthquakes, sensing them before they hit. My town was at the centre of one of the heaviest earthquakes recorded, but I didn't live there at the time, this was back in 2012. But I did experience a few earthquakes, one was in the middle of the night, and I woke seconds before it hit. I sensed it. I was like 'Whoa!' I heard similar stories from other people too. Experiencing the earthquake is one thing, but knowing that people cause them, is something else.

SISSEL

I'm still busy with the question of the role the sensing body has in archiving a nature-culture event such as the man-made earthquake. Throughout this research, I was also visiting a very physical archive, *The Core Sample Storage Warehouse* where all the core samples taken from the Netherlands must be stored by law. They're mostly used for the analysis of gas or oil content, so you can look at the specific sand constellations in the core to find out where the gas is hiding. This way of examining the data was a very sanitized version of the man-made earthquakes. It felt on the one hand very unapproachable, while at the same time it was an archive readily available in the public domain.

A member of the Chorus comes forward. The circle has been disfigured by now, with many members moving around as if concentrating on their own individual thoughts. All whilst listening and sometimes stopping to make a comment out loud.

CHORUS, ONE

We change landscapes based on human needs, so should we then think about the cultural aspects of the landscape?

CHORUS, TWO

The landscape in the Netherlands reflects the mindset of Dutch culture. For example, when you see the Netherlands from the window of a plane, there are an abundance of canals and dykes crossing the country. When you see this you know that you are above the Netherlands. Of course, it has to do with the necessity of making artificial land on top of ground that was once underwater, but doesn't this also show how Dutch people are pragmatic and direct? This is something that you can see in the landscape. Which came first: the mentality or the landscape?

CHORUS, THREE

It's a new kind of nature. It's now a cultural landscape.

Bert addresses the crowd from the stage, everyone stops moving and turns to listen, his expertise shines to the forefront.

BERT

cleaning his glasses

Here in Friesland, we say there was first the landscape – sea, water, earth, and then came the mentality. Maybe you know the word mienskip[9] or community. We're very proud of the idea that because of the things that we had to build, for instance the dykes, we had to find a way for people to work together. Community in the Netherlands, in Friesland especially, is strong. We have that aspect of the landscape being made by man, getting people to work, to develop a common vision of what they should do, and in which direction the land should be developed.

9 Mienskip: Bert Looper and Lieselot Van Damme, *Foreword*, Paragraphs 7 and 8.

From behind, Flora takes to the stage, but with cautiousness, not wanting to step on anyone's toes. Still she holds her ground and shares the spotlight with Bert.

FLORA

If I may interject, I think I disagree with your line of thinking. You are telling us this story about *mienskip* and Frisian community as if it was a historical fact, but I feel we should be careful when we characterize "a people" like that, so strongly conditioned by geography. I'm not saying that dykes were not built, instead I'm pointing at the danger of characterizing a commons as if we know exactly what it entails, as if it was a thing we can define, or even worse, as if it was defined some time ago, and now we can feel proud of, or just deal with the consequences. It might be more of a myth[10], and that is actually disempowering.

10 Myth-making: Flora Reznik, *Of Asymmetrical legs, scars, infrastructures and exile*, Paragraphs 12 and 13.

If I understand correctly, in your text you attack the fact that Frisian poetic tradition doesn't allow us to see contemporary reality, because the images that it created are fixed in our heads, blurring our sight. When you mention that it is urgent that poets take off the "Arcadian glasses", I understood that you aim to dismantle myths, and in this way approach the concrete reality that surrounds us with clearer vision[11]. What I find in the concrete reality is that a commons is not something that pre-exists, but is something that needs to be built, constructed, re-imagined, re-named, with all the complexities and dynamism that a task like that entails, each and every time an encounter occurs.

11 Mythical poetry: See Bert Looper, Unknown words, unknown grounds. Language, landscape, and memory, Paragraphs 10 and 11.

BERT

What I want to say is that I think you can see in Friesland and maybe elsewhere in the Netherlands that we are constantly creating mythical landscapes, in which a specific aspect of a landscape (real or fictional) is valued positively and adopted in the collective imaginary as an element around which the national identity is formed. We discovered the Frisian landscape in the 19th century as a new form of identity. The village and the countryside, not the urban culture, is what has been valued, so when urbanization and rationalization of the agricultural area destroyed the countryside of the 70s and 80s, we discovered the Wadden Sea. The Wadden Sea is our new mythical heritage, onto which we project all of our desires and longing for reflection. And so, each time we reconstruct the mythical landscape, first in the countryside, then in the sea, especially in Friesland, and maybe also in the rest of the Netherlands, because what are we without them? We need them. We are not going back to a mythical landscape, but over and over we are creating new mythical landscapes. I don't know why, it's like our horizon. Empty green spaces that extend into the horizon, that's our mythical landscape now in Friesland. I think it has to do with our wanting to escape from crowds, from traffic, from the city, so every time again we create a new mythical landscape that we can project our deepest desires onto. But this particular myth, the one about the green fields, is detrimental in favouring biodiversity, which is what we really need.

With these abstract spectacles, we can no longer see what's *actually* going on around us. We have Obe Postma, the great Frisian poet, in our minds, we have this mythical relationship between man and landscape. When you read the poetry of Obe Postma, it's only about the positive aspects of landscape and not the reality of the situation. We idealize the images he evokes and the associated language he writes with here in Friesland, and maybe other parts of the Netherlands too, if not the whole of Europe. Language is therefore an instrument for great literature, but not a way to be engaged with everything that is happening now. Literature is not always discussing our decline and ecological crisis, or at least I don't find that the case very often.

CHORUS

interjecting

Now we are talking about a common cultural vision of a landscape, the Dutch and Frisians transforming basic elements into a cultural/communal landscape, but I am wondering: Are there examples of cross-cultural, or cross-linguistic variations in the constitution of and naming of geographical features?

Silence. Only a chewing noise can be heard. It's masharu eating earth in the back. Before anyone can think of an example, Andrej jumps back up onto the stage and begins to speak.

ANDREJ

talking quickly

Russian cognitive scientists from the 1930s, most famously Vykotsky, but in this case, Luria, conducted an experiment: these scientists handed out cards to illiterate peasants, trying to understand their classification capacity. They wanted to know how people pair things. They would give out four cards with apples, potatoes, knives, and gardening hoes on them.

This experiment is interesting because the illiterate peasant would immediately pair the apple with the knife. They were then asked, "How would a foolish person pair them?" They replied, "It's obvious, foolish people would put potatoes and apples together."

This capacity to classify abstract terms is something that we take for granted, but I think it's culturally determined, to a certain extent.

Theun, still sitting on the edge of the stage, offers his own take on the topic.

THEUN

Our taxonomies of plants and animals are also culturally determined. Classifying species is quite difficult. It's a task of translation from observation to agreements in the scientific community, etc. For example, some scientists say: "oh well, actually I think that the orange spots on this butterfly make it a separate species." The butterfly receives a new name and biodiversity increases.

In Holland, biodiversity is higher in a city, like Amsterdam, than outside of the city. Significantly higher in fact. Not just because there are lots of plants from shops, but also because the nutrient load on the landscape is much lower than in the countryside. Industrial agriculture diminishes plant diversity more than urbanization.

Bert, standing behind him, clears his throat. The spotlight returns to his face.

BERT

Indeed, in our Dutch landscape we had a lot of biodiversity. Maybe not nature in the strict sense, but this biodiversity is gone. When you now go through Friesland, you will say 'What a beautiful green region." I grew up in the late fifties and sixties, then Friesland was not green at all. It was yellow, it was blue, it was red. There were different colours. And now people think if it's green, then that's nature, that's okay, because we have abstract images in our mind of what landscape should be, about horizon, about room, space and so on. We do not know the names of the plants, the trees, we don't have the names so we can't see.

A member of the Chorus leans with their elbow resting on the stage, they have a question, a comment, all the above and more on their mind.

CHORUS, ONE

I moved to Friesland five years ago from Amsterdam. We live in the countryside in a little village. We really did think we were going to live in this romantic green area. Now that we live here, we realize that we are in a green industrial area. We didn't notice this when we were living in Amsterdam.

I'm studying the landscape, not only in the Netherlands, but also in other regions where nature is still very prevalent, where there is still a lot of nature in general. Friesland is a cultural landscape, and so nature has disappeared. The landscape is still there, but it is what the Dutch literally made of it. To compare, in Norway, you feel that nature is still very much around you and it's bigger than you, but in the Netherlands, you will never have that experience because maybe it was never there in the first place.

BERT

We need to get rid of this admiration for the "green" Dutch landscape. Such a simple way of describing landscape is too abstract and stays at a superficial level. Between 2002–2006 a group of researchers compiled a dictionary called *Home Ground: Language for an American Landscape*. Their ambition was to retrieve, define and organize the nearly thousand terms and words for the topography specific to the United States. Their aim was, as Lopez wrote in his introduction to the book, to recall and explore language because he believed that using language to say more clearly and precisely what we mean would bring us a certain kind of relief and would draw us closer to our own landscapes. It is language, he concluded, that keeps us from slipping off into abstract space. The book's ethical presumption was that having such a language at hand was vital for two reasons: because it allows us to speak clearly about such places and because it encourages the kinds of allegiance with one's place that would also go by the name of love, of which might arise care and goodwill. The research team located the terms, defined them, and illustrated them through usages in American literature, science, and art. The result is a kind of sustained prose poem, exquisite in its precision and its metaphors. '*Home Ground*' does not so much define as it evokes, or rather it defines through evocation. Thus, this dictionary proceeds to lyrically renew a language of place.

I think because we lose the landscape, we also lose the words to be specific in what we see. You must see with words, otherwise you won't see anything.

Andrej shakes his head before placing it into his hands. He finally resolves to take a stand. Reaching his hand out for the microphone, the spotlight is slow to move in his direction.

ANDREJ

I am boldly disagreeing with the idea that we need language to see.

All eyes are on him now, and suddenly the atmosphere has become thick as butter.

ANDREJ

I think it's the other way around. We shouldn't confuse the priority of engagement with the priority of language. It seems to me that if you disregard the material substrates that we speak of, then it's almost impossible to describe what's going wrong.

A member of the Chorus coughs.

CHORUS

Do we need to see in order to have language, then?

BERT

I think we have a definition problem because what you said is regarding *ground*. We are talking about landscape, and landscape is of course a mental construction with ground as the basis for this fundamental position. I think the vocabulary that we had or have for nature provides us with a frame of reference. When you want to change the landscape, you must have some notion of what it could be. You must have the words, otherwise, in what direction will you go?

ANDREJ

turning to Bert

Do you equate thinking with language? Can't there be thinking without language?

The Chorus erupts into a clamour of voices. The pit looks like a boiling pot. Three members of the Chorus stand and speak at once.

CHORUS, ONE

The first thing you have to learn when drawing is to let go of all the concepts that you had.

CHORUS, TWO

You have to let go of all the words otherwise you can't make the drawings.

CHORUS, THREE

If you draw you don't necessarily need to think, you just do.

ANDREJ

Now we are making a case for the problem of the hegemony of language. The real mystery is the body and not the mind in this kind of relation. One does not decide to think differently voluntarily. You can't sit and decide, "I'm going to think differently." It doesn't work like that. It must be provoked. A process of inflicting a violent shock to our thoughts[12].

12 Provocation for thought: See Andrej Radman, *Groundless Grounds*, Paragraphs 1 and 5 and Affected thought: Flora Reznik, *Of Asymmetrical legs, scars, infrastructures and exile*, Paragraph 14.

CHORUS, ONE

Thinking cannot be dissociated from embodied experience.

CHORUS, TWO

But new thoughts are always a *new combination* of thoughts that already existed.

CHORUS, THREE

I have a problem with the word 'new'.

ANDREJ

I would argue that thinking isn't composed of already existing concepts, subsuming everything you have seen under the concept that it is already there. It's about rewiring the brain, inducing the possibility of generating general discomfort and encounter. It is the opposite of recognition[13].

13 Anti-representationalist approach to perception: See Andrej Radman, *Groundless Grounds*, Paragraph 4, and reference note 7, and Flora Reznik, *Of Asymmetrical legs, scars, infrastructures and exile*, Paragraphs 12 and 21.

Flora raises her hand, but the spotlight remains on Andrej and takes a while to find her, so she starts speaking in the dark.

FLORA

Thought is a product, it is never original, but it would be too sad to say that it is only ever a combination of already existing thoughts. If that were the case, then there would never be anything new under the sun. I do think we can speak of something new appearing, as long as we don't conceive it as an isolated thought, born from itself. What's new is always something other than thought. Thought comes after. Thought is provoked by something else. Thought is not a matter of thinking: its source, cause, and hopefully aim, are something else. This "something else", by definition exceeds thought, so it cannot be properly thought, it hasn't been thought yet, i.e., it is not recognizable. This is nevertheless what makes us think what we think, and we are trying to think that experience. What forces us to think and what we cannot think, pushes, and expands the borders of the thinkable.

Sissel pops her head into the discussion.

SISSEL

One does not sit in a chair to think.

ANDREJ

Exactly true. To think (differently) we must feel (differently) that which pushes us. To feel differently we must be open to a (confrontational) encounter, beyond re-cognition, beyond counting on what we already know.

CHORUS, ONE

If you cannot see what is happening, or really feel something, you have to let go of the notions of what you think you know, because these ideas set up a boundary that limits you.

CHORUS, TWO

Yet the more words about food you know, the more you can taste, for example. When you have a background in a specific field, you can appreciate it more.

CHORUS, ONE

But I think you can also be open to things, and the more you're open to perceiving, the more you perceive. If someone doesn't have a large vocabulary, it doesn't mean they can't be open to complex experiences. Maybe they cannot use words to describe their experiences in the moment but they can still express them in other ways.

FLORA

This leads me to think that maybe, not instead of, but parallel to, thinking of this opposition between language and experience, we can also go into the problem of translation[14]. I have a big problem with this notion of 'common ground', as if language was only and primarily a communication tool for referring to a shared ground. If we think of language always as translation, and take seriously the risk of miscommunication or even of language as something irreducible only to the use of this communicative tool, then the problem shifts. It's not only about first remembering words or having a language at hand to then engage in a new way with the world, we must start by acknowledging that we have some shared words but we are not a community of speakers, so we need to see what we can make of this. It's always first a task of making an experience accessible for others. Along similar lines to what was now mentioned, the case of someone "expressing an experience in a different way". This comes from a text by Ettiene Balibar, a French philosopher. He had this idea of language as translation. He was not attempting to say what language is, he was not saying 'ontologically language is translation', it's more of a proposition, a political proposition. If I have to put this into my own simple words, I would say: it is about not assuming I understand you, it is instead about introducing a bit of doubt into my own certainties, always double, triple checking, engaging in the cumbersome labour of constantly having to paraphrase, to ask for clarifications, but never trusting that "this" is the one definition of a certain thing. This technique is one that must be used by everyone if they intend to be heard in the public arena. Conversation can become a bit slow, for sure.

14 Translation: See Flora Reznik, *Of Asymmetrical legs, scars, infrastructures and exile,* Paragraphs 23 to 26.

BERT

It's a complicated relationship, language and reality. What's happening right now when you only know the word "green" for a landscape, is that in the future it will only be green. But what if we want to have it yellow, blue, red, then we need the sentences that remind us of the fact that the landscape can be as diverse as it once was.

FLORA

We can agree on a common goal. But we can't take for granted that we understand each other, that we share a language and that this can be a main tool to build a common ground. Sounds difficult, but that agreement has to happen without the certainty that we all share the meaning of the words in which the same agreement is drafted, so to say. Sounds like a vicious circle, but I think it is a virtuous one. It is the opportunity for the appearance of relevant difference. Otherwise, we miss the focus on what's most urgent: the fact that often we don't understand each other. And this is not something that can be solved. Perhaps it is even something we should cherish and protect. Agreements are negotiated, not consensuated. I hope I'm making myself clear, that everyone understands my words according to the intention I am giving them. But it's most likely not the case.

Theun stands up and wanders around the stage as the Chorus settles back into their places, forming a circle again. The lighting softens. The spotlight follows Theun as he continues to walk and talk.

THEUN

My friend once invited two men from Papua New Guinea who had never been outside of the forest, to come to Amsterdam. The stories from this encounter are great. The thing they were most scared of were dogs on leashes, because in the forest, not even the most dangerous animal is on a leash. "These small dogs must be incredible beasts!", they would say. These men came to Holland on an airplane, and they described it like a dream involving a huge bird. They adapted their language to a situation they didn't know.

A member of the Chorus comments, and others follow.

CHORUS, ONE

They described their experience in a poetic way.

CHORUS, TWO, TO BERT

Perhaps poets are no longer describing the landscape that you would like to be described. I mean poets are describing landscapes, but perhaps not the natural world.

CHORUS, THREE

But is it really meaningful to long for this mythical description that is no longer there, or shall we find new ways to define it?

CHORUS, ONE

I think when you want to approach the notion of nature, in the end you always turn towards mythical ways of describing it. We can't go back to these mythical descriptions because they don't exist anymore.

CHORUS, TWO

Well, there is nature, but it's a new nature.

THEUN

still wandering around the stage

I think in the end we can say that we should worry not only necessarily about looking out for nature, but about looking to engage with nature.

Let me present a case. Two scientists study a coastal bird and want to see what its influences on the local shellfish population are. It seems to be a really simple question, but it completely snowballs, because they start to study this type of bird, and they say, "oh, it behaved differently, maybe it was the weather ... yeah it was probably the weather". And they discover individual differences between birds, each may have slightly different feeding habits, so how do we deal with that? These individual birds also differ every year. So before you know it, the question is completely unanswerable. They conclude that our understanding of nature might be better aimed at refining questions than finding answers. What if nature is too complex for us to understand? How do you then protect something that you can't understand? When I asked my friends in the rainforest, "How can we protect what we can't understand?" They say, "well Theun, that's called love."

CHORUS

in unison

LOVE!

MODERATOR

Well, well, well, isn't that nice. I think it's time for a break.

From behind the stage a smell of coffee and chocolate can be detected. The Chorus seems to suddenly notice it, and as if they were taken by their noses, exit the pit by the side doors.

The contributors leave the stage, looking slightly tired, but cheerful.

3

THE RELATION AS GROUND WORK

STEPPING BEYOND THE DICHOTOMIES THAT LIMIT US

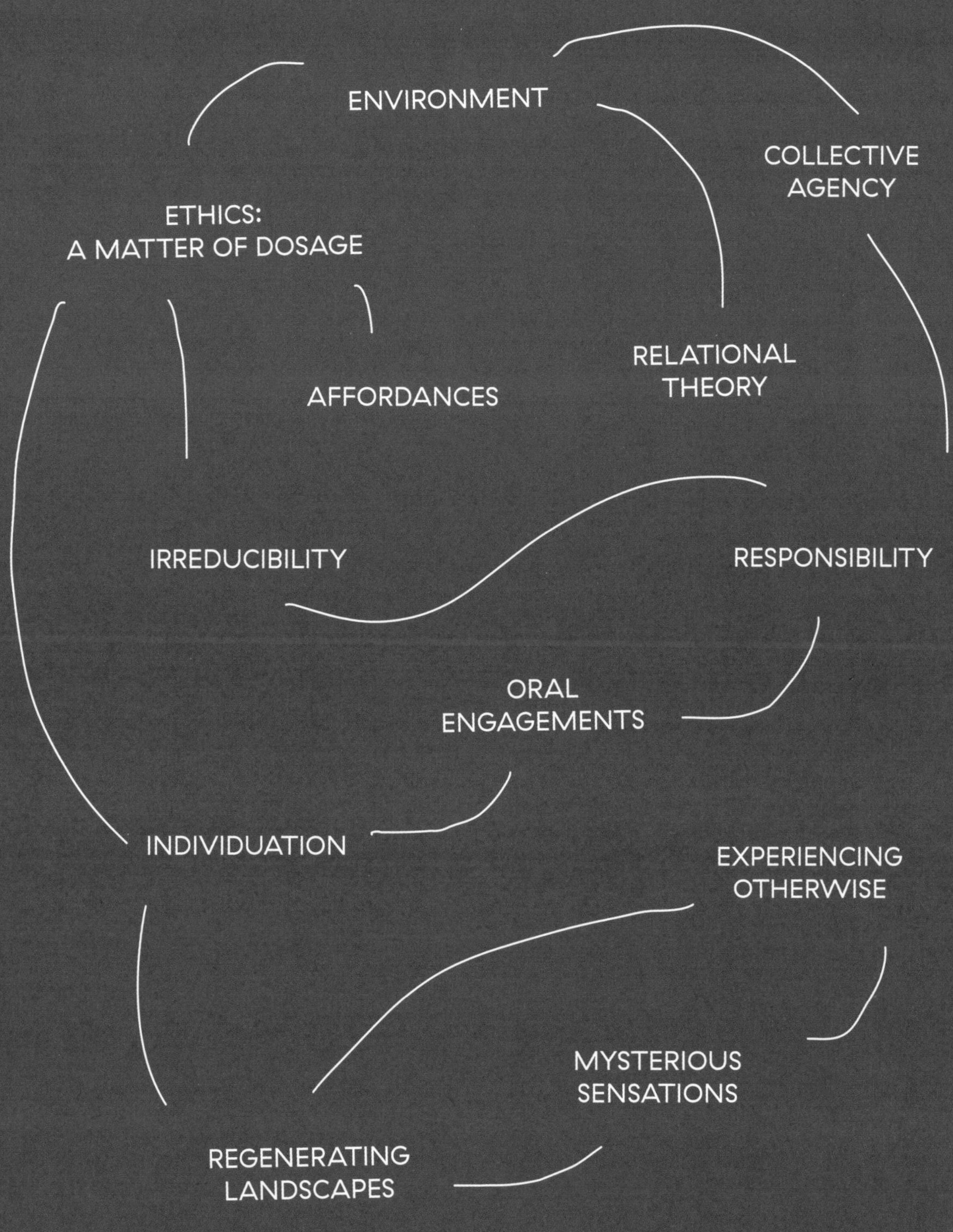
ENVIRONMENT
COLLECTIVE AGENCY
ETHICS: A MATTER OF DOSAGE
RELATIONAL THEORY
AFFORDANCES
IRREDUCIBILITY
RESPONSIBILITY
ORAL ENGAGEMENTS
INDIVIDUATION
EXPERIENCING OTHERWISE
MYSTERIOUS SENSATIONS
REGENERATING LANDSCAPES

Lights gradually brighten from the walls in hues of green and blue and a warm light shines upon the centre stage, which is still empty. The contributors enter the stage through the back doors and walk around freely. The Chorus is already in their location, feeling renewed. Finally, the Moderator enters the space and stands on an elevated surface among the Chorus members.

MODERATOR

After having discussed in depth issues regarding how naming our landscape affects our way of relating to it, or vice versa, it is time we take a careful look at how those engagements emerge. What else is at play beyond our good intentions, beyond our goggles that only see the green on the fields? It is time we get our feet in the mud of ecological theory.

Sissel twirls to centre stage, her dress billowing.

SISSEL

For us to even start dealing with the problems that we have created as part of an environmental ecology we must first consider how this is intimately entangled with our social and mental ecologies. Particularly how we perceive change within our close environments and how that affects us on a social and mental level.

Ecology is not just something we call the natural world. It also encompasses our social relationships and the constructions that we build through them. It also includes our mental worlds and how we connect to each other mentally as a form of ecology.

Andrej, approaching Sissel's place on the stage and stopping once she notices

SISSEL

continuing to walk around the stage

Ecological thought is really about irreducibility.

It's not the subject that has the point of view, but rather it's the point of view that produces the subject. You are undergoing an experience and then, and only then, do you realize that there must be a 'Me', a something, a centre to this experience. It's not just you pre-existing, it's through experience that you consume space, and then you realize: Oh, there is this going on?

But having the subject as a product is not disempowering. On the contrary, the subject becomes embedded in a network of relations. This is inscribed in the tradition of radical empiricism[1]. This perspective proposes that not only do we manifest things and their relations, but we can also tap into the deepest sea, beyond actual relations. To tackle this, we need to think that things, call them objects, subjects, or whatever, are in constant movement towards becoming something else, something that is not here and now (the 'here and now' is what we call "actual". What is not here and now but nevertheless exists and can produce effects, is called "virtual").

1 Radical empiricism: See Andrej Radman, *Groundless grounds*, Paragraphs 18 and 19.

The Chorus, who was quietly listening, is awakened by one extremely soft voice that speaks from among them. They might have been speaking for a while, but they are only now noticed. They seem to be drifting in thought, in turn unaware that anybody is listening.

CHORUS

Taking relations into account, I wonder... If you see two events and understand their causal connection, that might only be one of the myriads of possible relations at play, there are more possibilities that are not happening but could happen. When building digital interfaces, designers follow the principle that affordances should be made obvious and explicit, which is the space between the stimulus and response. Nudging users is easy when actions are constrained by design. How can architects and designers create space, or the ground, for freedom and subversions when neoliberal pressures push us in the opposite direction?

This member of the chorus suddenly realizes that a circle has formed around them and that they are capturing the attention of everyone. Caught by shyness, they run away from the center and join main the circle, whose center now remains empty, like a question without an answer. After some moments, Andrej starts walking tangentially away from the circle, and a light follows him as he speaks.

ANDREJ

Gregory Bateson, an anthropologist and cybernetist, talks about 'play'. You cannot play with a snake, a snake is fully interested in stimulus-response[2]. If you step on it, it bites you. With cats, it's something different. He says that the catnip is not a bite, it's exploration, the cat knows that it's not really biting, it's something else, it qualifies as a kind of thinking, because in play, I'm not really as I am now. Let's pretend this is a space where we can disregard the stimulus response. I just nip, I don't bite.

2 Stimulus/Response: See Andrej Radman, *Groundless grounds*, Paragraph 24.

The crowd breaks the circle and disperses.

ANDREJ

Linear causality is a very, very, very rare and special case of non-linear causality. DeLanda says to talk about non-linear causality is the same as talking about non-elephant zoology.

CHORUS

But how can these unexpected events be created?

ANDREJ

We can approach it by defining 'homophily': the idea is the homogenous neighbourhood, where the same or the similar begets the same. For example: When you are shopping online and you buy a book, you immediately get this message that says: "People like you read these books. They also bought these books." So if you want to be like people like you, you also order those books.

Bernard Tschumi wrote many years ago a sentence that resonates with me to this day. He says: „Architecture seems to survive when it saves its nature by negating the form that society expects of it.“ An example of this is Fast and Furious. Fulfilling the promise, or catering to the need that is expressed in 'Fast and Furious One, Fast and Furious Two, Fast and Furious Three, Fast and Furious...', you have your audience, the audience is fully formed, waiting for a Fast and Furious Seven, Eight.

Combating homophily cannot be achieved through diversification, it's not about the different, it's about the difference that makes a difference. I don't think heterogeneity is about diversity. Diversity is always a given. We then have to think about how the given is given.

We should think of 'affordances'[3]: risks and opportunities that are discovered or built in around us. Not what is expected, like a consequence that can be foreseen in the cause in front of our eyes. Radically novel events.

3 Affordance: See Andrej Radman, *Groundless grounds*, Paragraphs 13, 24 and 25.

A member of the Chorus runs towards the microphone in such a rush it was as if their question had an expiration date.

CHORUS, ONE

out of breath

Can you explain something quickly to me? What is an example of affordance and where can it be useful?

ANDREJ

smiling

Certainly. One example is sitting ability. The capacity to use what is known as a chair, so you can sit on it. It's completely relational because to figure out how to design sitting ability, you must take into account material properties of the structure, as well as how we use it and all of its variations, alongside all the kinds of heights of people, their weights, and so on. It attunes you to that. Rather than thinking about the chair you think about a wholeness.

Topologically an object is closed. In landscape terms, it is the figure that touches the ground, but with the environment the ground figure breaks up because it keeps changing all the time.

SISSEL

her steps marking the rhythm of her speech

I feel like it relates a lot to the work that my partner Jonathan and I make together. We try to create ways of mapping perception of an environment that is constantly undergoing change. We try to create mapping technologies that enhance rather than reduce the sense of constant change felt by the body when experiencing a new environment.

We created 'sensory collection devices', gloves which were picking up the electro-dermal activity of our autonomic nervous system. The device shows that the electric signals that the body is sending are in direct connection with the effective impact that the world has on us.

But we also tried to challenge ourselves a little bit in terms of how we experience this kind of environment or any kind of environment and by nudging or challenging the way we have been culturally and evolutionarily conditioned to experience an environment.

Another one of the technologies we developed is 'peripheral vision goggles'[4]. The way that they work is that they challenge the way that we've been conditioned to look in a linear perspective and they try to attune us to what is going on around us. Technology really challenges the way that I experience the world and makes me more disoriented, but also more attuned to other kinds of sensing.

4 Peripheral vision: See Sissel Marie Tonn, *Daily Research*, Paragraph 14.

ANDREJ

raising a finger into the air

You were emphasizing what I mentioned at the beginning as irreductionism. You cannot reduce either of the ecologies to any of them. The social, the mental and the environmental: none of them stands alone nor can one be explained by another. So what we have is the psyche, society, and the environment itself. Of course it's just three examples but it could even be three hundred and three, it doesn't really matter. That's irreductionism. Everything has changed into a new condition, so there is no going back.

SISSEL

walking around mounds of dirt

When I was working in the North, I was adopting coping mechanisms because I didn't know what to do with all this information. I was oversaturated with sensation. And I needed to find ways to recalibrate the way that I looked at things, so the peripheral vision exercise is something that I do when I cycle or run. I try to look at the movements that I have in the periphery of my eyes rather than just zooming into a subject with my linear gaze. To try to look at all these strange tricks of perception and find the greatest potential in them.

It's an incredibly exciting practice to always try and think of what's happening in your peripheral vision that you're usually blocking out because you're used to only focusing on what's in front of you. Or to even just think of the kinds of sensory expression that you are constantly filtering out, and how you can get in touch with those different aspects of experience.

Especially the membrane of my body. The outline of my body, and how I think about this outline becomes more or less a boundary or more or less permeable, changing the way that I relate to the environment, which is constantly changing as well.

A member of the Chorus raises their hand ever so politely.

CHORUS, ONE

to Sissel

Ehem... What's the point of trying to see otherwise?

SISSEL

It's more about ways of experiencing otherwise, it could be whatever way differs from your current bodily state and it just offers a space to explore that. It's something you can train. You can create these kinds of training grounds for sensing different layers that are barely there, and noticing the relations of the different spheres at play. For instance, some of the earthquakes that we are using in the installation are very soft, so the installation isn't like an earthquake simulator. It's more a training ground for attuning to these gradations of sensation that in a way are really important for our survival. It is these small changes that make us adapt and actively perceive things.

Making art is all about making choices. Choices of what you choose to pay attention to, and what you choose to transmit and the way that you compose how you've experienced a particular subject. For a year, I had been busy with this question of when you experience an environmental change within your close surroundings, how does that make that environment and the connections, the interrelationship with that environment more present? How can I grasp onto that sense of presence and make it more tangible?

The case I studied through this piece was not just a series of earthquakes. It became a social phenomenon. People gathered and created an alternative way of representing what is happening in Groningen. The social, the environmental and the mental ecologies were completely entangled.

Theun stands across the stage and takes a microphone, starting a new tangent within the discussion, his mind already making the connection to something else entirely.

THEUN

A thought comes to mind. I am thinking of the European narrative of the role of humans, which is often defined by opposing wilderness and nature to technology, for example agriculture. We are rediscovering that there are actually a lot of in-between things, between wilderness and human domination.

When the first English people reached Australia, they described it as a park, not just a small park. Everywhere along the coast when they came off the ships looked to them like a park. That's thousands of kilometres. They wondered, how are so many parks possible with such a small population? Bill Gammage makes the point that the entire continent was indeed like a park, and it was managed by the Aboriginals, not in the sense of farming, but by fire regimes, and although 'managing the land' may be the wrong word, 'attending' might be more appropriate. The Aboriginals shaped it with different fire regimes. You burn it every five years, twenty years, or every century, and when you do this, you produce different habitats. This was a very sustainable thing to do.

We're now in a dominant narrative where humans are destructive; we are a technological species, and these technologies are evil. I think it might be a nice change to think of ourselves as a fire regime, because we are also uniquely gifted.

A light bulb effect flashes above Andrej's head.

ANDREJ

This echoes with the idea of ecology ethics as opposed to morality. Morality is eternal, it is good versus evil. When it comes to ecology it's a matter of dosage, it's a matter of mutation, it's a matter of how much. You put a little bit of phosphorus into the soil, it helps plants, it nourishes them. You put a little more in, and you poison it. Then the question becomes not if this is evil or good, it becomes a question of how much.

THEUN

And I think that knowledge about what dosage is appropriate in a specific context comes from engaging with the environment. I work with the notion of 'environmental literacy': an understanding of your environment that comes from engagement.

I usually travel to do fieldwork[5]. 'Fieldwork' suggests that you are always in the field, in reality, field work could be a field, but it could also be anywhere. I work with groups of people, and this has become very important to the form of the fieldwork. It is increasingly taking the form of research programs that last maybe a year followed by a few sessions directly in the landscape, in an area, in a place with a group that seems well selected to engage with the research question. It is radical non-isolation: you're not split from the environment, you're not split from the other person, you're in a space where you're let's say, not at home or you're not really behind your own desk. With radical non-isolation you get, hopefully, non-isolation of thoughts and acts. And then the idea is that when you work in such a place, you can engage with local complexity by placing yourself in the full complexity of it and then you're not talking about some abstract nature, or some abstract industry or whatever it is, you're talking about whatever is around you and you're talking with it. In fieldwork you're really exposed.

5 Fieldwork: See Theun Karelse, *Machine Wilderness*, Paragraph 8.

The people that I visit in India for fieldwork work with plants. They're ordinary people, living on a nondescript hill that used to be a plantation and one person became interested in the orchids that grow on top of other plants, they are sort of epiphytes, they grow on branches. So this person wanted to know how plants grow if their roots don't grow in the ground. He then saw other plants that were similar but living on a different tree. Some of the orchids live on some trees and others on different trees, some orchids on one hill are different from the orchids on another hill.

From an interest in a single plant this idea sort of snowballed. This was forty years ago. It's just a group of local people that collected many endangered plants from roadsides, from all kinds of places, they taught themselves how to keep those plants alive, how to multiply them and by looking where they found them, they could sort of figure it out, okay this plant lives in this kind of an environment, etc.

When you have all these plants you can rebuild those environments. Slowly the hill that was once a tea plantation became a rainforest again. I would say there are now hundreds of species of plants on a hill that don't exist anywhere else that anyone knows of. It wasn't started because they wanted to save the world, or because they knew a lot about plants, but just because they were interested.

masharu, who had disappeared without anyone noticing, walks back onto the stage through a back door, pushing a trolley. The trolly contains a collection of earth samples.

MASHARU

I also travel a lot in relation to my practice. I have been collecting edible earth from many different places. I collect earth that is being eaten. Samples can be clay or chalk or other kinds of stone or sand, if they are eaten by communities or at least one other person then they can enter the collection, this is the basis for my collection[6]. Right now, I have samples from twenty-five countries and there are more than two hundred and fifty different samples. And I eat it too. I exchange samples and that's how my collection grows. It's an oral engagement. I am very curious to know how you each engage with earth.

6 Museum of Edible Earth: See masharu, *Museum of Edible Earth*, Paragraphs 13 and 14.

masharu passes around earth samples.

MASHARU

About my background. I come from Russia. I was originally attracted to eating chalk, so I was going to the most appropriate places to locate it, for instance chalk mountains, which are also sacred places. They sell the chalk from these mountains at churches. At one chalk mountain I was at a women's monastery so I had to wear particular clothes, a skirt, and a headscarf, otherwise I could not enter. The goal was to collect this chalk not to visit the sacred place. The interesting thing is that this same chalk is sold online as an edible product. Exactly the same chalks, in Europe and in the United States, are sold as edible products from Russia. They even have the pictures of the same church on their websites. I'm going to pass the chalk around for you to try. There you go.

Samples pass from hand to hand among the members of the Chorus. Some dare to taste, some get rid of it quickly as if it was a hot pebble that burned against their skin.

Theun finishes his bite and stands up from a squatting position with an open, curious smile on his face.

THEUN

Do you eat much?

MASHARU

Yes, actually, I eat it a lot. If you google, you can find people eating a lot, a lot, a lot of it. Sometimes they spit it out in the garbage afterwards so we don't see that in reality they didn't swallow.

Amongst the chomping and chewing of samples, a member of the Chorus stands to ask a direct question. Many seem to want to ask something as well, but they wait patiently.

CHORUS, ONE

How did this start?

MASHARU

Ever since childhood I've wanted to eat earth. It's a desire that I've had, an urge.

More hands raise, curiosity rumbling through the ranks of the Chorus and contributors alike.

MASHARU

handing out another sample

This one is from Guatemala, it is produced by a church too. I'm going to send it around. You can try it, if you really want to bite the tablet then that is also okay.

CHORUS, ONE

The Church makes this?

MASHARU

Yes, and they eat the whole tablet for spiritual cleansing.

masharu inspects each of the remaining samples before choosing the next one to share.

masharu, handing out another sample: This tablet is sold on the market. If you buy a pack, it is cheaper.

The Chorus erupts in laughter.

MASHARU

They come in different designs. Mary, roses, Jesus as well as combinations of this imagery.

The laughter continues.

MASHARU

I would guess this comes from a quarry.

I will move on to the next samples. This one from Suriname is called Pimba. It is used for eating or on the skin or else putting in a space dedicated to the ancestors. It's sold on the market and in big quantities. Sometimes people eat one bag of these, one plastic bag per day.

CHORUS

in unison

Whoa!

CHORUS, TWO

I was curious if it does something to your psyche? Like your body and your experience with yourself?

MASHARU

Well, that is a good question. I'm not sure. I did experiment. I eat maybe ten grams per day, twenty grams per day maximum. It's not like I eat two kilos. I did an experiment where I tried to eat a lot of this every day and tried to eat as little food and as much clay as possible. What I learned is that I didn't need to use toilet paper anymore.

More and more laughter fills the stage.

MASHARU

It was very smooth, my sculpture. So this is for sure what it does, I'm not sure about the rest of my body. I mean it can have a cleansing effect, but it can also take out iron from the body, or some other minerals. I actually have very little iron already, even before I started this. This being said, eating it can also have many desirable effects. About this I'm still very curious, I cannot really tell yet exactly what the benefits are, I would like to do more experimenting. I want to eat a lot of clay and see if I will survive or how well it will go. I haven't done this type of self–experimentation yet, so these are only my guesses.

I'm going to send this sample around.

CHORUS, THREE

savouring a piece of earth

It's so soft.

MASHARU

So, I'm moving onto other samples. This one is from Nigeria. They are a bit hard to bite, so just see how you feel about it. You can also smell them. They're smoked. The smell is really nice, I think.

CHORUS, FOUR

I got a barbecue rock.

CHORUS, FIVE

Smells good. I could eat that.

MASHARU

Coming back to the Netherlands, there's a church named after Sint Gerlach. People used to eat earth from this place in the 13th Century because miracles were happening there. The grave of Sint Gerlach is in the church, so there is not really any earth on the grave itself, but there is still some sand under it and in exchange for donations, you can get these little bags of sand. It's still supposed to be for eating, so I went in the church and took pictures, and I asked some people working for the church how they can continue doing this, because this earth isn't even from the grave, and they said that they church can make any earth sacred.

A member of the Chorus falls out of their seat laughing and others follow suit, rolling on the ground, perhaps intoxicated?

CHORUS, SIX

holding their tummy and managing to talk through the giggles

The church makes this?

MASHARU

Yes, and they eat the whole tablet for spiritual cleansing.

The same chorus member stops laughing and sits crossed legged on the floor, suddenly taken in deep thought. masharu passes around another specimen.

CHORUS, SEVEN

speaking directly to masharu

I had an experience of eating earth, it was some sort of Westernized normal kind of earth eating, a healing earth that you can eat when you have problems with your stomach. It came with a powder, and I ate that, and I had a reaction of resistance and almost puked, and now that I have tried the earth samples you brought along, I found them so much more delicious. I was really impressed, the smell of it, and then, the different tastes. Some were sweet and others saltier and crunchier. I got really into it. So yeah, thank you for this experience.

CHORUS, EIGHT

Are there examples of other animal species that eat earth?

MASHARU

Yes, there are many, and there are also scientific publications about animals eating earth. Off the top of my head the animals that eat it would be elephants, parrots, dogs.

THEUN

poking his head into the discussion

Cows.

MASHARU

Yes, cows also. I think pigs as well, right?

THEUN

Yeah, I guess.

CHORUS

in unison

They have to.

THEUN

Yeah, their food is in the earth.

MASHARU

Monkeys, for sure. There are more animals.

CHORUS, EIGHT

How could I start out as a new earth enthusiast? What can you tell me as an amateur?

MASHARU

smiling brightly

When I tried it for the first time, I was very enthusiastic, but I was totally resisting, my body was not handling it well. It just couldn't. But the second chalk was perhaps better, but still it was really the same sensation, like crushed medicines, a paracetamol when you don't swallow it immediately and you have this almost sick feeling. That was the second time and then I stopped. Until I found clay. It's my favourite. Maybe you can try different types until you find the one that is for you.

And I guess it's up to you how you take it. Are you brave enough to go out and start eating what you find? If not, you can also go online and buy different types of edible clays. It's very easy to do. You can also take some samples now and just experience it for yourself. There are also some people who have said they get some kind of psychedelic experience from eating this earth. It's like an experience of going back into the cave for a moment. So maybe you can experiment with it.

Another member of the Chorus, whilst picking their teeth, asks for a fresh glass of water and gurgles loudly into the microphone before speaking.

CHORUS, NINE

I cannot stand it at all. The feeling in my mouth. This sandy grain. I'm surprised. I really cannot stand it at all. My whole body resists it. I'm surprised that it had such a strong effect on me. It just ugh, I'm resisting it. It's not for me. But I'm surprised. I didn't expect it. I was very enthusiastic about your stories, and I went to try the first piece and I really felt ‚ugh!' I hate the feeling in my mouth of these little grains.

MASHARU

I once gave a workshop with students, interdisciplinary students at the University of Amsterdam. There were three students in the group who felt the same. In some places that I go, especially engaging with communities that know more about this tradition, they never have these kinds of reactions. So I'm wondering, in Western society we don't we touch ground anymore in our daily life. Is this disconnect what causes such strong adverse reactions?

CHORUS, NINE

My life is here in the countryside. So I really am in the ground every day.

MASHARU

You are very in touch with the earth. But you still have this reaction to it when it is inside your mouth.

CHORUS, NINE

The texture. When it was a soft stone, like the Pimba, it didn't really bother me, but those with a more sandy, rough texture, they really reminded me of when I don't wash my spinach properly, which is a bad experience... especially when it crunches in your mouth. It's a mystery, I wonder where this dislike comes from. It really surprised me; I wasn't expecting it.

Flora inspects a piece of earth in her hand, takes a small nibble and then takes the stage to speak, addressing the chorus member who last spoke.

FLORA

I was quite triggered by that dislike towards the feeling of a certain kind of earth in the mouth. It made me think that what emerges as solid reality has roots somewhere else, another sphere of reality that even though it's not material, is nevertheless powerful. There is a feedback loop between the actual and the virtual, – the virtual being what we cannot comprehend or recognize, what pushes us to come to reality. The metaphor of the tip of the iceberg is handy here: the virtual is what is underwater, and the tip is the real, supported and affected by all that is underneath, which is in constant flux. They are connected; there is an area that is blurry, a threshold... where the water doesn't let you see if it is the tip or if it is underwater. It's not linear causation, one affects the other and vice versa.

ANDREJ

speaking without a pause between his words

Technically, the virtual is fully real (albeit incorporeal). The loop is between the actual (the manifest) and the virtual (the potential where the principle of non-contradiction does not apply). As Spinoza put it, we don't know what a body can do. Not because we are ignorant, but because it depends on the (ever-contingent) relation. Ecology teaches us that one should never go below the relation. As Bateson's (tongue-in-cheek) expression goes, that would be like studying the anatomy of half a chicken.

Take the style of Baroque. It's not like there was a moment when all the major figures got together, you know, and come together in a setting like this to decide what are the features of the Baroque. It is something that comes out of a collective endeavour, it's something that starts in a way of rearranging material in the realm of actuality, but this setup produces an effect, and this effect is material, yet incorporeal. It doesn't have a body. And at that point the effect is incorporeal, and it becomes a quasi-cause. It has a capacity to limit the degrees of freedom and the level of action. It's like falling in love, it's as if something exists alongside the lovers and yet it has the capacity to make them do this or that. So, yes, it's the non-linear causality.

You know, I'm saying this and I'm glad to address this because very often we pride ourselves in what is known as the level of the virtual, and many people come to us and say this level of the virtual, where does it come from? It's completely detached from the actual. No, it's actually this wonderful, strange loop where the actual state of affairs produces an effect and that effect in turn becomes a quasi-cause that functions at the level of the virtual, so then suddenly we stretch the circle from the Renaissance to become an ellipse in the Baroque. It's not a law, and nobody has asked for this, but suddenly there is a convergence in mathematics and the arts, we start thinking about the infinite, we have manipulated reality to produce a new virtuality that now produces a new existence, a new mode of life, literally a mode of life. There is nothing natural about it, it's completely artificial, it's always contingent historically, but once it's there, it's determining the degrees of freedom, it is contingently obligatory. There is nothing necessary about this set up, the fact that I am sitting here, addressing you.

CHORUS

Are perception and experience key to understanding our environment?

ANDREJ

Action and perception are never ever to be disentangled because they are completely inseparable. Gregory Bateson always says that it makes no sense to study the smallest grain of reality: it is the organism plus its environment.

The room brightens with daylight, everyone swallows their last bites. A fresh breeze blows through the room and the Chorus stands.

THEUN

standing front and centre on the stage:

I have an idea for an activity, and for it we can all play outside for a little bit. A change of context, exposed to something other than this confined space.

Everyone exits the theatre. In the fields surrounding it, natural light gives a different coloured tone to the skins and clothes, and the eyes take a little time to adjust to the new setting. The fresh air brushes everyone's hair. The murmur of the grass being combed by the breeze fills the space.

Theun observes everyone, and patiently waits for the right moment to speak.

THEUN

Please choose an animal you'd want to perceive the world through. What is that animal's experience like?

A piano is heard at a distance playing a playful tune. Elephant (x2). Dog. Rabbit (x5). Rat. Black Bird. Owl. Chameleon. Lion (x3). Butterfly. Squirrel. Cat. Stork. Mouse. Badger. Snake. Turtle. Frogs (x3). For fifteen minutes the cast dances and plays around on the stage. Once this time is finished, they come back inside the theatre. They sit on the ground in the pit in silence. They seem transformed and relaxed.

THEUN

Now what did you all experience outside?

A rabbit takes a microphone.

RABBIT
I was surprised by how many people chose the rabbit.

THEUN
You didn't get together, all the rabbits?

RABBIT
Yeah, we found each other.

THEUN
You shared your food?

RABBIT
Of course! We were very nice to each other.

DOG
I'm more sensitive with smells than when I am a human. Usually, I wouldn't care if I smelled a car. Now I would feel annoyed and try to get away from it. The church looks extra gigantic to me. There was a sculpture that looks like shit.

THEUN
You want to be existential.

ELEPHANT
I am the elephant, as you can see. I was like walking around and trying to crush all the shops.

THEUN
In fifteen minutes did you crush a lot here?

ELEPHANT
There are a lot of public artworks I really wanted to smash, but I couldn't.

CAT
I was a bit in doubt whether I should go inside where it's warm or outside where there are people, and it's a really nice group of people.

TURTLE
I decided to climb on the stairs.

THEUN
That took fifteen minutes?

TURTLE
My shell is very heavy.

The lights black out.

After a brief pause, the piano plays a quieter tune, the lights return, and the contributors are at centre stage. The members of the Chorus are in their regular clothes, humming to the tune.
The song ends abruptly. Sissel is the only one to remain in song. At last, she stops and stares at the Chorus.

SISSEL

We've all just experienced a kind of shock to our usual ways of experiencing. If there needs to be this kind of violent shock, a precursor to rewire the brain, can that realization happen unconsciously, or on a less cerebral plane?

ANDREJ

taking the microphone

Experience is in a big part unconscious, a realization might or might not be the result of a process, but the process can occur, nevertheless. Architecture often counts on that. There is one architectural feature, namely, the staircase that can do a lot of things, but whenever you see a public building, it is always, or very often, elevated slightly, and it's elevated precisely because it is a way of manipulating the capacity of the body to how we can encounter choices. Every church does that, every temple, you as a viewer leave the profane world down below and you elevate yourself. Through elevating, you see further, you feel empowered, you feel better, and now see this incredible view, but nevertheless, even if you know the secret, you've deciphered it, it works every single time.

Flora steps into the conversation.

FLORA

I can share a simple example, from a personal experience: what I study becomes goggles for my perspective. In the sense that the goggles are part of how I think and how I relate to what I make and what I experience: it is not only the content of my thoughts. Affordances are not only conscious thoughts. They are in things, as much as in for example a text, or the relationship between a text and a reader. So, I really try to reflect on that when I write, for example, but also when I read, and it's not like there is a logical consequence from one principle to a conclusion (that would be my conscious ideas guiding and ordering the text). Sometimes paragraphs, images, even rhythm, function as elements that co-exist and are related, that affect each other in a way that is not linear or explicit. I don't think I need to make every connection explicit. Perhaps if I leave them open, or if we leave them a little more in the shade, new associations can occur anytime.

There is, as I see it, a subtle parallel between what is "explicit" in discourse and what is actual, and between what is more evocative, poetic, elusive, open, and what is virtual. I believe in the power of a language and actions that are opaque, to trigger potential events, that otherwise would be occluded by clarity. I think this also has to do with the "widening of the gap" that Andrej was talking about.

A member of the Chorus comes from backstage holding a stepladder.

CHORUS, ONE

setting the ladder down and climbing to the top of it

This example of the staircase, it can be empowering, or you can feel better when you ascend it, but my first feeling is I feel manipulated or feel more humbled. It's also a way of distributing or executing power.

Ribal walks around the ladder and examines each step, precisely.

RIBAL

I don't like stairs. I don't really like the small steps. Stairs represent an unequal and closed society in my head.

Andrej sits on the bottom step, his chin in his hand.

ANDREJ

All of that is very possible indeed. Again, it is not a matter of good and evil, but a matter of dosage.

CHORUS, ONE

A person is not the same as another person, we are all different temporary configurations resulting from an infinite and ungraspable amount of variables that affect us and that we affect in turn.

ANDREJ

You have just basically explained the Affective turn. The shortest definition of Affect, and it comes from Spinoza: the capacity to affect and be affected in return.

Another member of the Chorus comes from backstage holding onto a giant question mark prop.

CHORUS, TWO

Do individuals have a responsibility to change the infrastructure i.e., fighting an algorithm that creates sameness? Mostly, I am thinking about strategies for changing perception. For example, in Sissel's work she works mostly from the individual side, but what I am concerned about is to ask these corporations, like Facebook, to let users create the parameters of the algorithm. This is something that we currently don't have any control over.

Andrej is softly pushed by the Chorus member holding the ladder, since he needs to take it. He stands, ponders at first, then answers quickly:

ANDREJ

It's not the subject that has a point of view, but rather it is the point of view that has its subject. The point of view pre-exists the subject. The very etymology of the word ‚subject' is wrong because it presupposes the sub, it is foundationalist, a 'substantionalist' concept of the subject. We should be called „super-ject" not the subject as the cause of events, but the subject as the effect. It's the subject as the effect, rather than the subject as the cause.

One does not start from either a fully constituted subject or object and then tries to figure out how they may or may not interact. This is what under the spectrum of realism goes under the concept of correlationalism. Individuals are the result of individuation, and it is an on-going process. Then it is not about figuring out how it is that the fully constituted subject and objects relate or interact, but how it is that we individuate differently[7].

7 No (fully constituted) subject: See Andrej Radman, *Groundless grounds*, Paragraphs 19 to 23.

There is a beautiful text by Didier, called "What is relational thinking?". He is a contemporary philosopher busy with articulating a new notion of nature, and in this text he says that most of our thought has relied upon the idea that the individual comes first and then collectivity follows, but if we think in terms of relational thinking, then the individual is the terminal point because there is never, ever such a thing as the individual, it's a process of production of individuation.

The Chorus erupts in murmurs, heckling nonsense as the stage turns black.

CHORUS, ONE

Oh no! Does that mean I've lost my point of view?!

CHORUS, TWO

But you gained access to a new cosmic set of relations. The old nature as something separate from the subject is no longer. Air, fungus, skyscrapers, spaghetti, my dead great grandparents, math, your nightmares, we are all in this together. Common sense will have to adapt.

CHORUS, ONE

I still want to gain a responsible perspective on how to fight the algorithms.

The performers rush out through the back doors, leaving the Chorus alone.

CHORUS, TWO

What does it mean to be responsible? Can an individual respond on behalf of just herself? Can responsibility be individual? Doesn't 'responding' imply a question asked by someone/something else? Who/what is asking? And is it addressing you, just you?

The members of the Chorus walk in circles, each around their own doubts. Slowly, the rhythms of the moving bodies start to sync, without any algorithm commanding this. The choreography becomes visible from above, and also from below, even as the members of the Chorus remain unaware. The lights fade out and the curtains drop.

4

MAKING SENSE AND COMMUNITY AS ARTIFACTS

HOW DOES A "WE" COME TO BE?

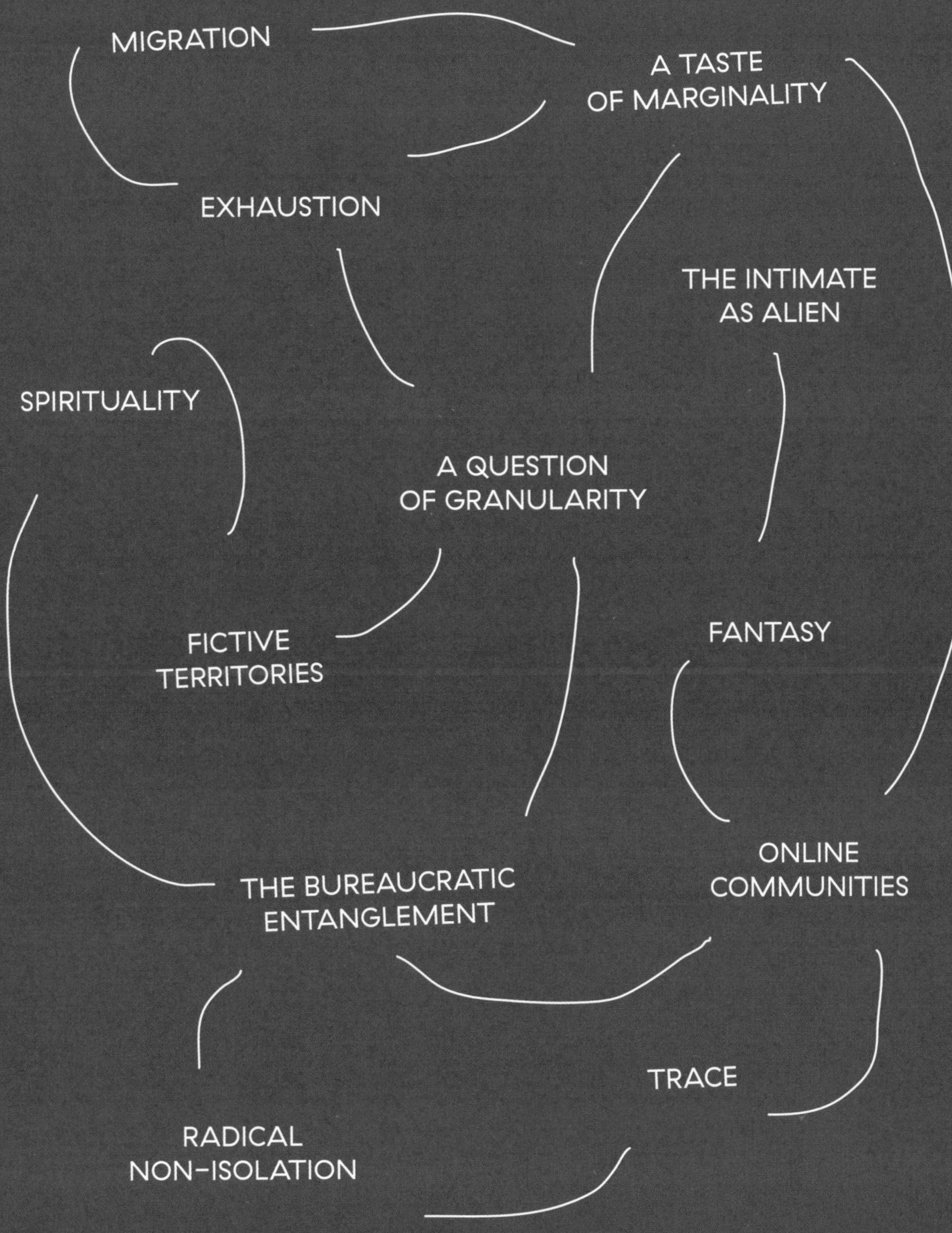
MIGRATION
A TASTE
OF MARGINALITY
EXHAUSTION
THE INTIMATE
AS ALIEN
SPIRITUALITY
A QUESTION
OF GRANULARITY
FICTIVE
TERRITORIES
FANTASY
ONLINE
COMMUNITIES
THE BUREAUCRATIC
ENTANGLEMENT
TRACE
RADICAL
NON-ISOLATION

The stage and the circle in front are pitch-black and empty. Overhead ominous music plays while the muffled sounds of steps tell us that the Chorus is entering the space. A strangely dark yet luminous mountain appears to grow from the flat surface of the pit, rising over everyone's heads. The Chorus climbs up the stairs onto the stage.
Once approaching the glowing mountain, they find it has no substance, it is a fantasia, a ghost of a mountain. It seems to be made of skin, but no one can touch it. It spins slowly as the Chorus circles the image at a synchronized rhythm.

FLORA

stepping into the light, interrupting people's explorations

I'm curious about what you all saw or what this triggered for you?

Members of the Chorus stop circling the image and disperse around the stage. They don't go back to the pit where they belong. Numerous microphones are passed around and shared.

CHORUS, ONE

I saw it as a landscape and at some points it seemed to be a solid sort of shape and at some points it seemed to be a surface that would be seen from under the water.

CHORUS, TWO

Looks like a glacier set free, drifting in space.

CHORUS, THREE

I felt a bit lonely. Like I was missing something.

CHORUS, FOUR

While I was looking at it, I saw the human I've been looking for.

FLORA

Indeed, I agree, it's very lonely there, but I hope this *landscape* intrigues you enough to want to sort of 'come down' and explore it. When you are there, stepping on the ground, a lot of questions may arise. You are surrounded by a lot of things, you're not alone anymore. Then you become immersed in an environment.

A member of the Chorus walks over the still moving image, disrupting the view. They stomp a single foot and point at the image.

CHORUS

But what is this? What is it made of?

FLORA

taking small steps towards the image

Ha! good question, I am wondering the same myself. I decided to work with the material trace[1] of a non-corporeal reality to see where it could lead me. This material, which is a weird mix of memories and emotions related to my brother and I, who are two separate persons but, at least in this specific case of the two of us, are so close that this distinction becomes a bit more confusing. I am also investigating subjectivity and intimacy.

The way I like to tackle the immaterial in my work is via something extremely concrete that somehow is connected but does not represent that immaterial realm. A particular scar located on my brother's leg evoked in me a dry riverbed. And so, I thought, what if you invert that? Then it's a chain of mountains. I found that very peculiar. Nowhere is a case study or a scientific law that says: when you invert a riverbed, you get a chain of mountains. Yet I sensed this was the case, and through artistic manipulation, there it was. And what does this tell me?

I made a silicone mould out of a human scar, my brother's scar. A mould is always the inversion of the thing that is being moulded. Instead of reproducing it, which would have involved making the positive, I stopped and stayed with the inversion. Repetition, but with a change. Technically, what you saw is an animation based on a photogrammetry model of the mould[2].

1 Trace: See Flora Reznik, *Of Asymmetrical legs, scars, infrastructures and exile*, Paragraphs 12 and 14.

2 On the process of making the art piece: See Flora Reznik, *Of Asymmetrical legs, scars, infrastructures and exile*, Paragraphs 1 and 5.

A member of the Chorus steps towards the image and raises their hand, the microphone crackling.

CHORUS

Has your brother seen your work? What does he think of it?

FLORA

her steps slowly turning into a dance

I had a conversation, yes. I involved him from the beginning and told him that I was planning to do this. And yeah, he said yes. Just "yes, sure, no problem". But that's the thing, I don't really believe so much in what people say. There are hidden layers of meaning, in us and in things, that I believe escape language. Something deeper resists representation in language, and we need other tools to work on that.

He also had the chance to participate during the making of the piece. He was present when I made the mould. That moment was very special. When we held the silicone mould in our hands, it was quite a moment, like he could hold his scar in his own hands, and it was the first time he was ever granted a different perspective on it. To touch it, like a blind person would touch a texture... there was a level of feeling or understanding that had nothing to do with anything he or I had experienced before or that we could put into words. The subtitles of the video are a fictionalization of a conversation we had, but the wording represents something other than what we call ordinary language. If anything, it is a poetic language, which doesn't represent, it evokes, it takes you somewhere else.[3]

This project seems to come back to a book I read many years ago, *The beast and the Sovereign* by J. Derrida. In this book, the sense came like waves that won't resolve completely, but rather the waves accumulate, a bit like sediment. The waves brought sediments; information passed a bit unnoticed[4]. At first all this information didn't seem to make any sense because it wasn't linear. Usually

3 Conversation between Flora Reznik and her brother: See Flora Reznik, *Of Asymmetrical legs, scars, infrastructures and exile*, Following Paragraph 5.

4 The beast and the Sovereign and Sense like waves: See Flora Reznik, *Of Asymmetrical legs, scars, infrastructures and exile*, Paragraph 27.

the 'meta' part of a text comes at the beginning, like a preliminary explanation, but this book isn't like that.

CHORUS

How can one try to make sense of an experience that occupies a blurry point in time and that cannot be pinned down? What is the difference between making sense and interpreting?

FLORA

I want to emphasize the *making,* which is connected to a collective endeavour, and it really involves building, working with materials, constructing, and it's not only a description of something else that already exists, that is given to a mind that interprets. It's something that I have to make because it doesn't really exist.

This work was a way to approach this personal experience, but also at the same time to investigate a form of experience that goes beyond the human capacity of understanding.

Something similar in a sense to Sissel's work, right?

The members of the Chorus rearrange on the stage as the mountain disappears, leaving an empty space. They separate into two groups on each side of the stage, and finally return in an orderly manner to the circular pit. Sissel takes centre stage.

SISSEL

My text Daily Research also deals with something that appears like a blurry, not well-defined experience. It is an attempt to gather all of these messed up and non-linear thoughts and experiences from my time in the North after I developed a concussion that obscured my cognitive capacities. I mixed them into an imaginative story of a person getting hit in the head and becoming sensorially exhausted by this phenomenon of man-made earthquakes[5].

But of course, I was also working with very real things. The way some people recalled their experiences of the earthquakes to me, really gave me the feeling that it was not just the earth moving, but it was also this sense of being abandoned for decades, not being taken seriously by the government or those that should be protecting you that creates this kind of earthquake of the mind.

5 Sensory exhaustion: Sissel Marie Tonn, Daily Research, Paragraphs 2 to 4 and 9.

A member of the Chorus separates from the group and speaks with uncertainty.

CHORUS

Does the project also somehow flow back to the people who live in the earthquake area?

SISSEL

It was developed for the museum as a gesture to think about how to place these kinds of events in the cultural institution.

We tried to choose specific earthquakes for our project that had this bureaucratic, almost bio-power quality to them. To find out what were the bureaucratic and social aspects around the event when some institution said: "this was the earthquake when there was no longer doubt that this was an issue in the country".

There were soft earthquakes when I was there, but I think I was either too busy or I was simply not well attuned enough to the earthquakes because I hadn't lived with them my whole life. My well-being wasn't threatened by them. On the other hand, myself, as much as the other residents of Groningen, in a big part, are also benefiting from the cause. For instance, I cook on gas.

CHORUS, ONE

almost shouting

There are so many different stakeholders, and no one wants to take responsibility!

CHORUS, TWO

I would suggest that the next step, the next level, would be to publish and to show your work in a different way: to have an active audience, to be able to hand it over to others, not as an artwork, but as a tool.

CHORUS, THREE

A dichotomy between an artwork and tool raises many interesting questions. But I'm wondering what is the difference between an artifact and a piece of art?

SISSEL

pausing before answering

A tool would help me to relate to the issue. Art can also fulfil that purpose, can't it?

The Chorus falls silent, all stepping backwards a little. Andrej steps forward and speaks.

ANDREJ

Both projects make me think of the idea of granularity when it comes to personal experiences. Basically, meaning *how to find the grain*. That this work is not idiosyncratic, it's not about your brother or your head concussion, nor is it about every brother or head concussion in the world, there is a danger in making it biographical and idiosyncratic that it only describes one singular person and no one else whatsoever. The other danger is making it all-too-inclusive and therefore a codifying moment where it's universal.

FLORA

clearing her throat

Experience is always definitely somewhere in between the individual and the universal. Neither one nor the other. Is it a mix of more things, like me, my brother, the scar, other people, *and* the tools that we make to try to understand things?

But I believe in the power of the personal story, even if it is a fiction or a tool to make new fictions. It conveys a certain strength. In regard to a personal story there is nothing more to do than to believe it. You can't prove it. Hence the link to fiction or poetry.

And what would a community that honours and respects that element of uncertainty that represents the personal (as much as the personal in the other, a.k.a. a plural, diverse society) look like? On what grounds can it stand? Perhaps it is a fictive territory that we need to build together? Fictional in the sense that Sissel and I, and I think also Bert are working towards noticing what's missing, dealing with wounds, with concussions, with listening to the stories of others.

From the pit emerges the small round platform where the Moderator stands. The spotlight shines on her.

MODERATOR

We have one contributor that didn't submit a written text, but instead contributed photographs and this was his way of sharing his story. Ribal, may we have a look at your photographs?

The spotlight shines on Ribal's face.

RIBAL

laughing

Of course! You can also see them on Instagram[6].

6 Instagram handle: @rk_pho

Images appear on the walls of the stage.

MODERATOR

They are quite beautiful. These are scenic photographs of what the Netherlands looks like. Typical Dutch landscapes.

A member of the Chorus stands and dusts off their hands before taking the microphone.

CHORUS, TO RIBAL

Is this how you perceive the Netherlands?

RIBAL

Yes. I really like The Netherlands. I take photographs of the architecture, which for me is the identity of the country. Architecture identifies a location.

The first thing that caught my attention when I moved here were the houses with sloped roofs. We don't have this feature in the Middle East, the brick pediment, the gable. It shows that it rains a lot here. Architecture really shows the connection with the environment and what people do in relation to it.

MODERATOR

Talking about that, maybe Flora can continue by telling us about her encounter with Ribal, a total stranger?

FLORA

sending a cheeky look to Ribal

Around three years ago, I was doing a residency with VGDH, traveling for a month and a half around Friesland. I was developing another project and one day I decided to take off, just wander around and not work. I was feeling very lonely, living in this bus all alone and traveling for more than a month and I had finished some part of my project somewhere in the East of Friesland. It wasn't an easy time, this month, and a half, but it was really, really spectacular, it puts you out there a lot. On this particular day I decided to take some time off for free time, so I was going to a vacation park that I saw on Google Maps to park this monstrous bus.

I'm en route there, and I see a guy that looks like a tourist, on a bike with a really big camera looking at the sheep and this was in the middle of nowhere. Some kilometres ahead lay the vacation park. It took me a long time to get to the vacation park driving at 20km/h (which was the max speed of the bus), and when I got there, he had arrived already. Then I think to myself "this guy probably speaks English" (a tool that not all, but many foreigners share). At the time I knew almost no Dutch, so the whole communication during my trip was a bit hard, but I thought "this guy must speak English, so I'll go and say hello." I go there and say, "Hello, I'm Flora. Do you want to be my friend for today?". And I offer my hand for a shake. "What are you doing here?" I asked.

RIBAL

Yeah, I was lost. I was on my bike, and I couldn't use my phone, it was out of power, and I didn't know how to get back. It was about six kilometres away from my place, where I was living at the time. Okay, so what will I do? I'll take some photos and then I will go back and try to find my way.

FLORA

It wasn't very clear if this vacation park was open or not.

RIBAL

It was fenced off. It looked like private property and I was afraid to go any closer because I didn't know what would happen.

FLORA

I didn't find it scary, so I led the way and got us in. Later on, we sat there in a park in front of a small lake, and he told me part of his story. He told me that he is an asylum seeker. Well, this was not the first thing he told me. First, we talked about his photography: he told me that was indeed how he had gotten lost, he had gone out to take some photographs and lost his way.

A member of the Chorus steps from stage left with a hand searching for a microphone.

CHORUS

But you were cycling around there and despite that nobody knew you were an asylum seeker?

RIBAL

Yeah.

More Chorus members step away from their ranks and join in on the questions. Microphones fall from above and the Chorus scramble to the floor, grabbing what they can.

CHORUS, ONE

That's kind of weird.

RIBAL

How would they know?

CHORUS, TWO

Yeah, I don't know. Nobody asked you anything? You didn't have any human contact?

RIBAL

No, this is why I like it here, actually.

CHORUS, THREE

Because everyone just leaves you alone?

RIBAL

Yes. I do have an ID that was given to me by the Dutch government, but for two and a half years, no one ever asked for my ID. Not one official, not a Policeman, no one, no one ever here in the Netherlands. I want to show my ID for something!

CHORUS, FOUR

No one asks you where you live?

RIBAL

No. Why would they? Do people ask you where you live when you walk along the street?

CHORUS, FIVE

I don't know, maybe when you have small talk with someone.

CHORUS, SIX

Yeah, like where are you heading to?

RIBAL

That doesn't happen to me here, people don't talk to me on the street very often. One day I was in Zwolle, and I was with my camera, and I was taking some photos and there was a man with a very big camera, for TV I think. It was the birthday of the King's mother. And he was talking, and I was like "No, no, no I don't speak Dutch". "Oh English, okay. Hi Hi. It is now the birthday of the queen, and do you want to say something?". I thought, I don't know her at all, so I said, "Happy Birthday". And then he asked me, "Are you a tourist, what are you here for?" And I said, "I'm a refugee" and he was like "okay, bye." This is the only time, the only person who really asked me a question on the street.

MODERATOR

In the village where you live, is the asylum seekers centre a blind spot for the rest of society? Do you experience it in this way?

RIBAL

Very much so. We are living in a normal neighbourhood. Our neighbours don't know what is going on inside the building. People don't know what's going on there or who is living there, so they have a very negative idea of it. The centre organizes an open day so people can walk in and see what's going on but people don't go. We are living in the same land, but really, we are separated.

The building used to be a prison. It has a fence, a high fence, I think it is five or six meters high. To go in or out, we go through the gate, there is security. From the outside, they think it's really closed, so no one goes in.

Because I am an architect, I can identify the oppressive side of the design. No matter what they do, even if you take down the bars, as they have by cutting them down, they're still there with the doors one next to the other in a row, and the small windows. There are traces and elements, they are still there. It's a prison. Even if you are free to go out, it's a prison.

So that's why I am always out. I just go there to sleep or if I have something official to do, a meeting or something like that, otherwise I am out.

Some of my photos, of all sorts of buildings in The Netherlands, also the ones where I live, have been featured in the newspaper and they write a small article on my photos and there was one comment, "What's going on there?"

The Chorus is calm, but more hands start to shoot into the air with questions for Ribal.

CHORUS, ONE

And why do you want to share your photographs?

RIBAL

First of all, it is to use newspapers and Instagram as media where I can show my photography to the outside world and receive comments and build a network, and secondly it is about expressing my feelings.

MODERATOR

Because you combine them with text, right?

RIBAL

Yes. Sometimes people get angry or sad or they have depression, and they express it in other ways, different ways. I choose this way of expressing my feelings.

CHORUS, TWO

So you're building a community whilst becoming part of a community and you are adapting to that community and keeping your individuality through your thoughts and your photos?

RIBAL

Yeah, through my photos I am part of a bigger community. A community I want to be part of. After my first post, after I started my new Instagram, I showed that I am a refugee, and I was a little bit afraid to say that to people. I found out that no, it's the same. I am Instagramming for the Art in the photos. They don't look at my personal situation, but it was better for me to tell people that I am in this situation, because they understand more about what is going on.

Photography and Instagram have been a kind of integration tool. I know a lot of photographers here and they are doing almost the same thing. Everyone is telling their followers their thoughts; they are expressing themselves in their own way. Everyone is doing the same, posting a nice photo, writing some nice quotes. Everyone, that is photographers that aren't professional. I mean I'm doing this as a hobby, I'm not getting money for it. I'm not selling the photos, it's just a space for self-expression, a lot of people do it like that. In many ways I'm a typical Dutch Instagram photographer.

And isn't that what really matters. It's politics that makes differences between people, but if you are sick and you go to a doctor, they can help you because we share the same anatomy, we have the same organs, we have the same everything. We cannot be differentiated just by borders and territories. I hope out of all of the new things coming, advancements in technology, through means of communication like social media, that these new inventions will bring us together.

A silence reigns for lengthy seconds. The Chorus has nothing to say - united in a shared sense of respect for the words this man has just said.

From the side of the stage masharu approaches Ribal.

MASHARU

You talked about your past life just now. Can you share with us what a place that you would like to live in would be like?

RIBAL

Yes, actually, I am the kind of person who doesn't like crowded areas because I've been living in a very crowded city, and I don't like it. I'd really like to live in a village. I don't like stairs. I don't really like small steps either. I like to be inside but not covered; I want the house to be made of as much glass as possible.

Besides that, I'd like to be safe, in a good community. And to be equal. Yes. I wish I can live like this, to be equal, to live equally to others because there is a lot of discrimination. Discrimination about nationality, about colour, but because people are used to experiencing it, we don't really describe it in detail very often, but I feel it here.

While all the heads are focused on Ribal, one member of the Chorus turns swiftly towards Theun, the neck movement propelled by a brilliant idea.

CHORUS, ONE

Theun, I have a question for you: could you talk about more practical tools for non-isolation? Maybe it can come in handy for all of us here.

THEUN

What I find really beneficial when I am in a place I don't know, is to have somebody with me that's local as part of the group. That's beneficial because if you're just a visitor, or if you're just a group of visitors and you don't know the area, and there is no one to ask questions to, then it can become superficial, or it can be hard to go beyond superficiality. So, it's great to have someone with you that has historic knowledge of geology, or of anything really. All of this helps.

The Chorus forms a line behind a microphone, a spontaneous form of organization to be better able to ask their questions and to be heard.

CHORUS, TWO

When you start fieldwork, do you begin with a question?

THEUN

I've found that the more open the question is, the better. I guess I talk to a lot of people about many things, but I don't directly ask them: "What do you think is the best way to take care of this endangered environment?" I talk to a lot of people that normally are not asked about certain things: when I'm in the forest with indigenous people I ask them what they think about Artificial Intelligence because what I notice is that people from indigenous backgrounds are asked about what it is like to be indigenous and not anything else really.

The member of the Chorus who asked the question goes to the back of the line. The person who was second in line is now ready to ask the next question:

CHORUS, THREE

Theun, I noticed in your text you say that fieldwork is a crucial ingredient for artistic practice. I think it goes beyond that, fieldwork is a crucial tool for human beings. It's about how we connect, about how we become aware of our environment.

CHORUS, FOUR

I want to return to your experience in the jungle and the villagers you interacted with there. I was wondering, what did you want to learn from the people in India, and did you offer something in return to their community?

THEUN

I've been documenting their work with plants. And now I am showing them the change that has taken place over the years they have been doing this, so it's actually quite informative. I ask them if they maybe have documentation from before I started and then they showed me documentation from, let's say, twenty-five years ago. A local from the forest helped me to find the same places to take a new photo. My friends would say, "Oh yeah, this plant has just grown beyond recognition." Or they would say, "Oh yeah that's true, we used to grow grasses there, indigenous grasses, why don't we do that anymore?"

When people ask, "Why are you going to India?" I always say, "I have friends there." Fieldwork is not only in faraway places. If I go to the fruit farm in Purmerend, it's the same thing as if I go to India. There I have a friend and he requires help when he goes to pick his apples. I really like to go with him, so I go there, and I learn. In that case, the exchange is quite straightforward, he gets someone to pick his apples.

The Chorus line continues as Theun stands at centre stage.
The other contributors fade to the background.

CHORUS

in unison

You don't just take, you always give something back.

CHORUS, FOUR

These groups have all of their own meanings and understandings of their world. So how do you go about it, as an outsider, finding a way into a world, a community? From my own experience as an anthropologist, I have found engaging in this way to have many barriers.

THEUN

nodding

How do *you* engage?

CHORUS, FOUR

I actually don't engage that much because of the confrontation it requires, but perhaps that also has to do with the topics I am dealing with. I am researching the management of the underground. In the end, for me, it would require confrontation that is going to limit me from understanding their perspective. So, I'm hiding in a way. I'm just playing along, getting information and then I take part in a research findings presentation and that's my moment to give feedback. You start to question certain practices, not necessarily because of judgement, but more to understand the paradoxes.

THEUN

Do you also engage with the people that live in an area, besides experts or managers?

CHORUS, FOUR

I tried, but engaging with people is the hardest part. I want to work with those who are the lowest in rank, the people that are actually digging, and it's very difficult. If you want to talk to these people, they are very suspicious of you. I'm a woman, I'm very educated and people working in the construction site, they are used to people like me watching them for control reasons, in some sort of evaluation process.

THEUN

Hmmm... that sounds difficult indeed. In any case, participation is a strong entry point. It's easier when it's not formalised by framing it as a project. When you are just visiting, and when you're just interested, and not quite sure what you're doing, I think it's easier to get an idea then. I think it helps to do things together, in an open-ended manner.

MODERATOR

to masharu

Perhaps masharu's tasting activities are a little bit like that? Please, let's sit all back in a circle.

The lights dim and the Chorus arranges itself towards the edges of the pit, leaving some space for the contributors. Everyone sits cross-legged in a circle in the pit. The stage is forgotten.

MASHARU

I'm not sure exactly how to go about it, and this uncertainty I think has to do with the fact that the country where I was born doesn't exist anymore and now that I have a new passport, I'm not sure if I'm really Russian. I don't look Russian. There are hundreds of ethnic groups even within Russia and all of my family looks different. Some look Asian, others look Roma, another one is Tatar, some look Jewish – one time I asked my mother and she said I have an aunt in Israel – but in general when I ask them anything they will say: "we are Russians, don't bother". I don't know exactly where my roots are. I am very confused, and even now as I live in the Netherlands, I will always be an immigrant, even after I received a Dutch passport. In Russia I'm not even part of the country anymore, so I think it has something to do with these different things.

This ideal to be based on the earth. There is a tradition of engaging with your land. *Your* land, and when we're engaging with other lands, what happens then? In Suriname, for example, it was very different. I came with my own earth, and I said, "Can I participate in the practice with my earth?" And everybody was saying yes to me because people would say it doesn't matter where it comes from. White earth symbolizes peace. Earth is viewed very differently there.

The Chorus murmurs amongst themselves and hands pop in the air.

CHORUS, ONE

It seems to me that on the one hand it is a very individual practice: some people have the need, they feel the urge to eat earth, and this is very particular. On the other hand, there is also a social side to it. Is there a relevance in doing it together? Engaging and eating earth together?

MASHARU

This is what I learned when I first started with this project. It is a very marginalized practice, so communities are formed because of it. I mean it is officially a mental disorder.

CHORUS

in unison

What?!

MASHARU

It's in the DSM–V[7] book for mental disorders. And it is a weird thing because this is an old tradition. It's very interesting how something normal in one culture becomes a psychological disorder in another culture. So, earth eating people here never tell their friends and family what they are doing. They are online communities for earth eaters.

7 DSM classification: See masharu, *Museum of Edible Earth*, Paragraph 5.

My friend who I travelled with to Ghana, she was born in Suriname, she started as an anthropologist and later she created a Facebook group for clay eaters. One must answer several questions before one can join the group. For example, you have to answer "what kind of earth do you eat? How is it for you?"

CHORUS, TWO

But sharing your information about how you've been eating the earth is not like doing it together. You aren't gathered around a table.

MASHARU

That's true. There are a lot of online communities, but this togetherness, I'm really looking for that in my practice. And here we are, for example. Because eating earth together is a lot more fun than doing it on your own. It's like anything else. It's much more fun to do it together. When I first gave a presentation at an exhibition on this project, I felt that a taboo was becoming normalized, and I had a warm feeling from it.

CHORUS, THREE

Maybe it's also really interesting to eat earth together in public.

MASHARU

I actually do it sometimes. I just come with earth and eat it with my friends. I'm doing it a lot now. On Instagram I talk to a lot of people, just like Ribal does, and on Facebook too, and some people say that they would actually like to have this in their country as well. Like these physical events and not just online communities.

A member of the Chorus eats a piece of stone and dances as their crunching is picked up by microphones hidden in the ground and played from the speakers.

CHORUS, FOUR

What kind of sensation does it give you to eat earth?

MASHARU

It feels like it's making me more grounded. I lack grounding in general. I'm too much in my own head. And when I eat earth, I become calm.

It's a practice that is connected to spirituality in many ways, about healing with earth. I use it not only internally, but also externally, for healing wounds on the skin. I would say that externally I see that it works, the clay especially. What I know for sure is that I have a craving and I then do something I want to do. If it's spiritual, if it's healing, I can obsess about it. It's a bit like people who like to have a glass of wine with dinner. I also like to remind myself that it may be my own fantasy.

Another member of the Chorus joins the dance amongst the mounds of earth.

CHORUS, FIVE

Fantasy is something you can believe in. If you eat earth from all different countries, I think you can compose your identity by eating different clays and that would be appealing to me. It is a sort of fantasy; it's a way of composing your own identity. You say that you look for the right composition of earth that you think represents you. Does this have something to do with different qualities that are inherently material or not? How do you make up such a composition?

MASHARU

Part of the performance is connected to migration, to migrant communities. Earth eating is a very marginalized practice in the Western World. This practice represents me as an immigrant and also as a person who has a desire to travel and actually become engaged with different earths. I am also really interested in the idea of exchange.

CHORUS, FIVE

I also fantasize about being a person that has meaningful exchanges with others, one who is here and there, but can still have a community. A community that is linked to earth but not to a single place.

A member of the chorus that hasn't taken to voicing their opinion until now, shyly approaches the discussion and asks to speak:

CHORUS, SIX

I like that idea. But I also like coming back home, and even more if someone that I know well and loves me waits for me with a warm meal.

The smell of coffee and chocolates, this time mixed with a soil-like fragrance, appears like a charm and drags everyone out via the side doors.

5

TERRITORY, CHANGE AND RECOGNITION

ADVENTURES AT THE MARGINS OF "WE"

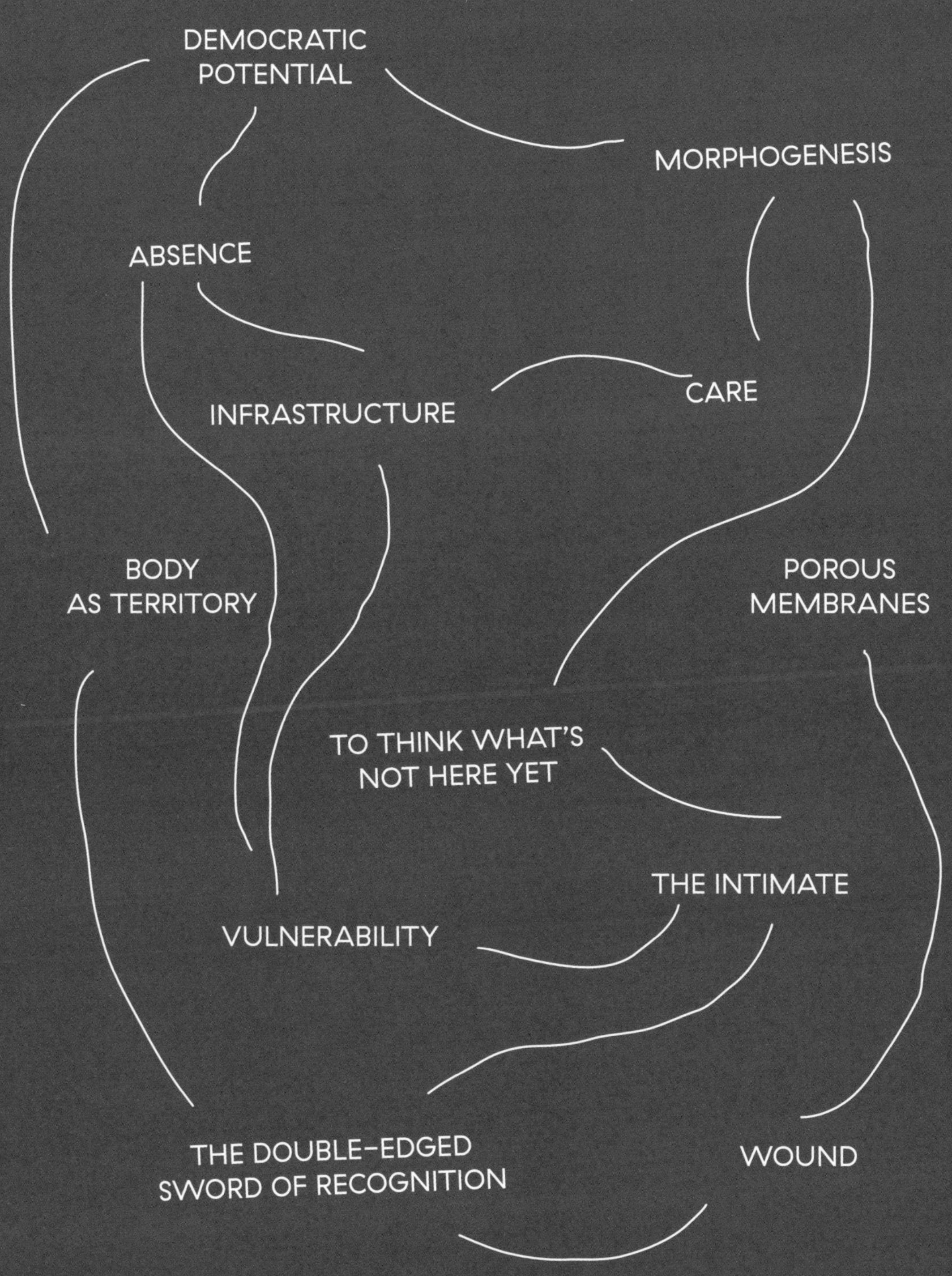
DEMOCRATIC POTENTIAL
MORPHOGENESIS
ABSENCE
CARE
INFRASTRUCTURE
BODY AS TERRITORY
POROUS MEMBRANES
TO THINK WHAT'S NOT HERE YET
THE INTIMATE
VULNERABILITY
THE DOUBLE-EDGED SWORD OF RECOGNITION
WOUND

A synthesizer produces a sound that evokes an outer space atmosphere: weightless, eerie yet soothing and inviting. The melody of a xylophone enters the room, guiding the contributors as they walk towards the stage with choreographed pace. The Chorus walks in a similar way, entering through the sides and climbing the few steps up to the stage. All mingle, taking seats on chairs that are grouped in pairs, facing each other, scattered across the stage.

A pair sit on the edge of the stage, almost falling off, a microphone in their hands.

CHORUS

looking at Andrej

Where does the ground end?

ANDREJ

I would say it doesn't. The process of territorialisation, which is to say circumscribing territory with a certain level of stability, builds habits that have a clear evolutionary advantage of being always on alert. It's a safe space. Territorialization has a feature, which is to circumscribe, to set a boundary. But it is always permeable. It has a centre, yet it also has to find a way of connecting to another territory. It must be open to the possibilities of de-territorialisation.

Deleuze has a lovely idea, he says if you think about territory, it's like when a child is just about to fall asleep and it's dark, and to produce a territory it starts to sing a song or hum a tune. This is a territorialisation activity.

CHORUS, ONE

This idea of territorialisation produces so many ideas about our bodies and the boundaries we make with other people. I am therefore wondering if any of the contributors could answer my question: *Is my body my own landscape or a part of others?*

Sissel enters the stage in a fabric bodysuit that she had constructed, her silhouette completely transformed. She crawls on the ground, adapting to a sudden lack of legs. She performs what could be called a dance, while everyone observes. Later she slowly emerges from the costume.

SISSEL

wearing a wide smile, messy red hair, and flushed cheeks

I'm really interested in thinking about the concept of the body as not being some kind of bounded, rational eye, but something more porous, much leakier. How do those constant exchanges challenge the way we think about our body in relation to the environment? These exchanges push us to look at this outline of the body. Not just starting from when we are born and when we die, or me being one person and the octopus being another person, but how the connections are operating.

I am also looking at it from an evolutionary point of view: what is the range of what we can sense and how does that affect our current situation and how can we learn from this ecology of technologies and other species or practices, or other artists or other fields?

FLORA

joining the discussion

It's very clear to me that the body is a very intimate realm and a sphere of solitude in terms of utter singularity, ownership, and responsibility. So much so, that sometimes it feels invaded, its boundaries trespassed. Yet at the same time, if you think about the body as the territory that we are and we inhabit, this is what connects us to others. What I'm pointing out here is not a statement about what the body is from a scientific point of view: it's an image or a concept, a proposal to think of one's body in this way. As a territorial body that is a socially malleable infrastructure, as opposed to something natural, immovable. Not only a surface on which we stand, but something that informs us and others. The territorial body, in this realm of intimacy, is at the same time what connects us to others, and what makes us vulnerable[1].

If a territory is something we need to share because of the proximity to others, (we need to share resources, we have to be able to deal with institutions, etc.,) and we said we can think of our bodies as entangled with the territories they inhabit, then it follows that our bodies are somehow also shared. They are not only our own. In *Totality and Infinite,* Levinas talks about the self as a house where the other is the first inhabitant. He frames it as a metaphysical and ethical statement, but I would like to think of it as a political statement: it is a decision we can take, together with others, to think of ourselves in this way. Or it can be a decision that we are forced to take. That's the basis, the force of the others that makes us open even when our tendency is to close up[2].

Jumping to a more observational statement (I wouldn't dare call it scientific), and back to referencing my own work, this is what a wound does all by itself. It closes its seams. It heals, while at the same time becoming a mark, a testimony of being originally open: not before, chronologically speaking, as if we were dealing with linear time, but fundamentally. This oscillation between territorialization and deterritorialization that Andrej mentioned, I think it's constitutional of how we are in society.

1 Vulnerability and Infrastructure: See Flora Reznik, Of Asymmetrical legs, scars, infrastructures and exile, Paragraphs 15 to 21.

2 Priority of alterity: See Flora Reznik, Of Asymmetrical legs, scars, infrastructures and exile, Paragraph 3.

CHORUS

to Flora

Is emptiness or a missing limb part of our landscape reality?

FLORA

It can be interesting to pay attention to the role of absence in what we call reality, if only to counterweight a simplistic idea of reality reduced to what is present in front of us. As if it was all of it there, ready to be re-presented in our heads. Speculative thought, for instance, doesn't work this way.

The notion of trace points to a structure of presence-absence as a fundamental structure of experience. A trace points to something else that is not there, a trace is a trace of something else. This concept of trace is from Derrida, and I kind of fell in love with it years ago. Much later I ended up making a project that took a year and a half to complete about scars, so it's interesting how things come together sometimes. Derrida works with the notion of "trace" not by making a definition of it, but by letting it mean everything that it can mean in any language spoken, in any real use it has. A trace is coincidentally a mark, like a scar[3]. Basically, if we are talking about marks, we are talking about marks on the ground, about marks in the mind, in the heart. We're talking about scars; we're talking about concepts of philosophy. A trace is a fissure on the present reality, it is what is going on that opens up to an *avenir,* which doesn't translate simply to *future*. We need to follow that path, and in following, we are also enhancing it, instead of resisting it.

3 Scar/trace: See Flora Reznik, Of Asymmetrical legs, scars, infrastructures and exile, Paragraphs 2 to 4.

A firework sparks over Andrej's head and he shoots a finger into the air.

ANDREJ

speaking quickly, yet again

The problem is when the mind tries to impose form onto what it considers an inert dumb matter, with no morphogenetic capacities, and for us these morphogenetic capacities are already there, they don't need us, but we might as well, you know, try to tease out something that is clearly not present. Not necessarily manifest, it takes a little bit of thinking.

FLORA

in conversation with Andrej

It makes no sense to only try to come to ideas that are fixed or stable (we don't think images, we move towards things that are in turn in movement). What is important is to go with our attention and agency towards that sphere of reality that is not stable, not present in one identifiable here and now. Better put: our agency should be destabilizing. We should be somehow noticing the potentiality in things. This porous outline of things, what makes solid not so solid i.e., the grey zone where something becomes something else, when things move further to new modes of being.

ANDREJ

smiling

Yes, spot on! Put succinctly, we counter-effectuate to re-singularize... or explore the potential that is not-as-yet-fully-tapped. You are right in claiming that this is crucial... the incorporeal yet real realm.

CHORUS, ONE

loudly

My English is not that good, but I want to say this: If we are talking about grey zones, I think about borders. Take the Dutch and the French border, everybody thinks that's normal. I think the world is not just lines on the maps, these are just definitions, how people are called or call themselves, concepts.

Ribal enters the stage with a chair in his hands. He places the sitting device off centre.

RIBAL

sitting very close to them

If we are talking about this in the context of the Netherlands, there is a territory where people who are called Dutch live and are all living in the same way. And then there are also more people living in the same place that don't get to live in the same way. You see it on the ground, not just in my mind. I can be Dutch in my mind, but this will not help me in real life. If I don‘t have the paper, I cannot stay. I cannot be here. This is my definition for it. I look at it not emotionally or philosophically, but practically.

I ask, are we connected to the land directly? Or is someone or something moving us to connect, or forcing us to connect to some area or some other place? Or even to disconnect?

A member of the Chorus steps into the spotlight, and after looking towards Ribal and then Flora, they speak. They are holding their hands as tight fists, almost trembling.

CHORUS, TWO

Ribal's experience upsets me so much. *Turning to Ribal.* We all saw your photographs, that‘s what matters. It looks like your quiet existence at the asylum centre must remain a secret, yet you are also trying to be part of Dutch society. You are here, but you are kept in a sort of limbo, inside and outside.

RIBAL

In the Netherlands I tend not to be recognized. This is why yesterday I said I am an architect because I have a degree, but I didn‘t mention photography because I don‘t have the recognition. I don‘t have a means of identification, an ID.

I was born in Abu Dhabi, and I lived there for thirty-five years, yet I‘m still not a citizen of the Arab Emirates. I don‘t belong there. Just because I don‘t have the papers. I lived there my whole life, but I was a foreigner until the very last moment and I had to leave because of the law.

Recently I got official papers from Lebanon, but it is very confusing, because you see that the document is in Lebanese, but inside it says I am Palestinian. When you are at the airport they are confused. „Where are you from? Are you Palestinian or are you Lebanese?“ It‘s a really confusing situation.

FLORA

while placing a chair next to Ribal and sitting on it, talking as she moves, making the last word coincide with her but touching the chair:

„Pas de loup"[4].

Flora makes a dramatic pause. People seem confused.

CHORUS

What?

4 Pas de loup: See Flora Reznik, On asymmetrical legs, scars, infrastructure and exile, Paragraph 27.

FLORA

It's in French, sorry for my lousy accent. Here ‚pas' is a negation, but it also means ‚step' or ‚passing'. Loup means wolf. The wolf is not there, but the wolf is also passing[5]. So, it's passing, but you don't get to see it passing, or you don't get to recognize it as it passes in front of you. Maybe you saw a shadow, or just felt the breeze it created. You can't re-present in your mind what's going on, you can't capture it. You can't represent it because it has never been fully present, or it didn't give itself to you fully. Not only is there an incapacity on the side of the observer, or even bad faith: there is also something that resists representation.

5 Passing: See Flora Reznik, On asymmetrical legs, scars, infrastructure and exile, Paragraph 17.

This is to say: representation, recognition, is a double-edged sword. It is something that can be granted to you, and then you get benefits, and it can be at the same time something you resist, strategically passing unnoticed, which can also have its benefits. In both cases it can happen to you without any degree of freedom. In any case, it's the result of a struggle, never simply a decision of the individual.

And if the wolf passed, even if unnoticed, a certain infrastructure was in place to allow that.

SISSEL

Can you talk about other appearances or ‚passings' of wolves in the tradition of Western thought?

FLORA

The wolf features as part of the mythical grounding origin of Western (political) culture: the wolf that breastfed Romulus and Remus, the twin protagonists of the story of the foundation of Rome, the "cradle of civilization", according to the Western tradition. Then the wolf appears many other times, the one that comes to mind now is in Hobbes, the image of the man-wolf, "man is the wolf of man", meaning he is very bad, and we should take measures to protect ourselves from ourselves, namely, we must create a repressive and all-powerful state to control us. (Parenthesis, I am a big fan of Hobbes, he is the first one to acknowledge this is only a useful fiction, which makes it at least contestable, as opposed to other thinkers of the time - and present times - who are fixated on an idea of nature, be it good, bad, or whatever, which is therefore not changeable nor arguable).

In the new „The Jungle Book" Disney movie from 2016, Akela appears in the film as the alpha wolf, the strong patriarch that has the sovereign power to accept Mowgli into the pack. When Mowgli starts using human tricks (technology), he decides he needs to leave the pack, as he has broken the Law of nature. When Akela is killed, Raksha, the adoptive mother wolf of Mowgli takes a prominent role, as someone who loves him and does not want him to leave, even if this breaks the rules. I found this really interesting, as a new take on the old figure of the wolf. These are all stories, myths, charged with ideology and the power given to them by repetition and reinforcement throughout history. They permeate popular culture, and even unexamined political assumptions and notions about society.

Judith Butler talks about the difference between recognition and apprehension[6]. There has to be a way of experiencing that is not yet, or perhaps not at

6 Recognition vs apprehension: See Flora Reznik, On asymmetrical legs, scars,

all, recognition or representation. Because a recognition is a representation, meaning it's something that comes back, that has been there before, in front of you, at hand. It was there, present, and then I can re-present it, name it, take an ID photo of it. A way of noticing something radically new or radically alien regarding certain standards, without being assimilated (meaning erased of its singularity), should be called something else. It calls for an agency that respects that singularity.

CHORUS, TWO

to Ribal

People don't see you, people don't want to see you sometimes. And there's a whole infrastructure of power and politics that allows that to happen.

Ribal remains silent.

FLORA

But we need to step carefully here. You wouldn't want to be seen in just any way. There has to be a way of relating that has to do with care, or perhaps that has to deal with conflict.

Amid conflict, if we are waiting to understand, we are too late. I'm trying to aim towards a discourse that diverts from the politics of recognition – or recognition only, because that presumes either mutual understanding (impossible) or patronizing, unilateral understanding (authoritarian).

Yet, there is nothing wrong in trying to understand, on the contrary. I see it as a way of reaching out, from a place of vulnerability, without guarantees.

CHORUS

I was wondering if vulnerability is critical for establishing a sense of place or for communication in general? Is it possible to participate in an environment as a vulnerable being?

FLORA

The proposition is that we're all vulnerable beings insofar we have bodies: all bodies need a network of support that extends to other people, but also the environment we contribute to shaping around us. It's a general condition, there would be no no-vulnerable being basically, not even a Sovereign, everything suffers (in the sense of affordance, of the capacity of being affected and affecting in turn), from stone to flesh, that is what it means to participate in an environment. But I'd like to point out that when we make general statements like this, it is a bit like with Levinas: it can be a metaphysical statement, but I personally don't want to say things about how the world is. I don't want to describe reality. I want to enact a difference. Because, and this is the other face of the same issue, some bodies are more precarious than others, because our political system distributes vulnerability disproportionally.

My statements are propositions, and in order for them to take place, they need to struggle in the political arena. The idea would be to admit: „I don't understand you. I don't know what you're saying." It is an issue related to the commons. As I said before, I think the commons is not a given, we don't have much in common in general, or rather, I'd like to focus on our differences, which make our ensemble rich, not tautological.

SISSEL

placing her seat some meters from Flora and Ribal

This just reminded me of another daily practice, or daily research that we've incorporated. John and I organized „The augmented attention Labs", and one of the activities we proposed, in collaboration with a research group in Berlin that works on embodiment and sound, explored how sound and movement can enhance the experience of being within a body. One of the tools that they brought was based on the concept of micro phenomenology, which is the research method for making quantitative analyses of experience. They showcased this interview method, and basically it entails sitting in front of a person and asking that person to pick one second of experience. It could be you just fiddling with that pen, and then through this interview method you uncover all the layers of experience of that one second of experience. At first, I'm sitting here, I'm fiddling with this pen, but as you go deeper and deeper, you notice all these layers of experience that you didn't pay attention to before because your brain filters them out, because otherwise you'd get constantly overwhelmed with experience and sensation, but that doesn't mean those experiences aren't there.

I remember just sitting and listening to this conversation and thinking that this had an immense democratic potential. I think again I want to stress that the sensation is also a political question. Who senses what? Who is forced to sense some things rather than others? I think this echoes Ribal's question, about if there's something moving us towards or away from engagement, or even if we are part of a movement, if we think of sensation as the link to an environment.

FLORA

Sissel mentioned two words at separate moments there, and at some point in my head they clicked together: *exhaustion* and *change*[7]. I felt that there could be a tension of values. We praise change in our culture. Everyone should be working hard, be creative, an entrepreneur. It goes along with this idea of progress and the self-made man, also with the tireless efforts of capitalism to atomise us. I think we live under this pressure, or at least I feel this pressure. There is this aspect of change that is socially regarded as positive, and counter to that there is exhaustion and numbness and not being able to feel anymore. I feel your work is tackling that and trying to avoid the numbness. I thought that was really interesting to explore on so many different levels. I don't know if anyone else has worked on or thought about exhaustion in all these different layers of reality like the mind, or the modes of exhaustion of the ground, of resources. Can't be a coincidence, all these things in processes of exhaustion, can it?

7 Exhaustion: See Sissel Marie Tonn, Daily Practice, Paragraphs 5 and 10.

CHORUS, THREE

Some of the most important people in my life are currently struggling with scars. Their bodies seek to heal, but they produce tissue that is tough. Tissue, which pulls together forcefully, inflicting pain and discomfort. I wonder if that can serve as a metaphor for political coalitions that have been atomized politically by neoliberalism, and existentially by this reaction to alterity. Which might in the end be the root of so many evils. If we can only hope to form these tough tissues that pull us together, that signifies healing, however uncomfortable and imperfect. Judith Butler sees vulnerability as a plausible foundation to solidarity, but proximity and interdependence are unwilled. In these times of extreme vulnerability, I constantly feel too anxious and tired and conflict avoidant to care for others beyond the domestic sphere while the world is clearly in need of the opposite actions. What do you think about escapism, resentment, and self-isolation as political emotions in times of extreme precarity? What do we do when care for the self and care for the world appear irreconcilable?

FLORA

I must say that the notion of self-care, in my opinion, is a dreadful commercial enterprise and it works towards enhancing isolation and atomism. To shield ourselves requires effort, and it drains us. But we become so used to it that we don't notice anymore. We are already open, it's only after that we try to close off. Of course, we might need rest, we might need to withdraw every once in a while, but care has to do with connection with others. An oscillation between these poles might be an option.

Solidarity sounds old fashioned. But in political terms, I still think that is what we need to work towards. It might be as rewarding as making new friends on the road on a lonely day.

CHORUS

What are the conditions that have produced us; a certain kind of society that can become so numb towards what surrounds us?

ANDREJ

running forward from the back of the stage

An example immediately comes to mind: *Delirious New York,* the book written in 1978 by Koolhaas. There he says, take the most technical of all the gadgets, namely an elevator: the elevator is almost like a seed that produced the skyscraper, because once you have the elevator you have the means of stacking a lot of floors on top of each other. First you have the elevator and now you have the possibility of fast vertical movement, so you have the capacity of going up in a very efficient way, and of living stacked on top of each other. Then that produces a culture of congestion; you have the possibility of putting together heterogeneous things, so we have two naked guys eating oysters on the 27th floor with their gloves on, and he says, „who could not love this?" Who could have invented this sort of thing? It's a metropolitan subject. It was not made for this, but now these possibilities appear.

The technology that has been used in the culture of congestion produces a certain kind of metropolitan subject. And now if you try to distinguish between the goals and the technical means and, to distinguish between the discursive and the non-discursive, between the *pathic* and the *ontic,* between this and that, you just can't. It's the whole thing that has produced this.

I think that we find ourselves in a moment where technology is faster than culture. Culture is lagging. So, we have to invent new categories, new theories to be able to keep up the pace and understand what is going on, and that in itself can be exhausting.

Everyone drops to the ground into what seems like a sudden collective death. After some moments, some of the bodies are seen to be rolling, stretching out limbs, producing guttural noises. Luckily it wasn't death, but a deep slumber.

Timpani boom with the power of thunder.

Everyone raises their heads and opens their eyes, looking in all directions. Then they fall again. Bodies start crawling.

One more boom suspends the movement. Everyone falls back to the ground, as if lacking joints and muscles. Some go through the floor of the stage and the pit and are never seen again.

Slowly, some manage to stand up.

The chorus jumps around, propelled by extremely strong pairs of legs that bend and extend with animal force. They spring over the sitting devices, they are hybrids that can live on the soil, in holes in the soil, in the water, in the air. They utter a strange song, the words aren't clear, yet the nimble dance is contagious. A freshness such as the one in the evening after it has rained, and the smell of wet dirt fill the space. The chorus continues jumping with an unearthly energy, or perhaps thanks to a well-deserved nap. No! They are being lifted, ungrounded. They levitate, they seem to have lost all sense of gravity. And the lights, once again, slowly blackout.

THE END

COLLECTED TEXTS

PREFACE

What follows is a compilation of texts written by a group of thinkers (the characters of the Script for a Synthetic Play[1]), accompanied by questions that, from one view can be seen as entry points to each text, from another as interferences. Each participant of the performative–symposium was invited to submit questions in response to the following texts prior to the event itself. It should also therefore be noted the texts were written in the months preceding the symposium. Originally, there were as many questions submitted as there were participants, what is presented in this publication is therefore only a selection. The questions are not necessarily answered by the texts, instead they aim to prompt more questions, alongside deeper patterns of reading that will oscillate through this section. Perhaps you, as reader, prefer to keep the questions in the periphery, to fully address them later, after the completion of the reading of the texts. In any case, the questions are included to remind us of the open and non–authoritarian spirit of these texts, and to encourage us to actively read between, next to, or after the lines.

The invitation that was sent out to the participants when they received the texts applies to any future reader, and therefore applies to *you*:

> *„Your participation, dear reader, is crucial. We'd like to propose that whilst we read and when we meet, we commit to really engaging in conversation: with the texts and later with others. It can be through words, or it can be through gestures. We might need to invent new tools for communication. Let us set aside the fear of not understanding or the anxiety of having everything clear at once: they are opportunities for learning. Read critically, not in a futile way, but in an honest way. Let the texts resonate in your mind and body, being attentive to what they do to you, how they play with your memories, thoughts, emotions, and to what you can do with them. You may hate a text; you may feel joy and the excitement of a new discovery. Texts are here for that to happen.*
>
> *We can use texts as spaces for encounters with others, and even with ourselves in a novel way. An encounter can be quite a peculiar thing, both passive and active, both careful and violent. Let us be strong and gentle. Let us share our half–baked opinions, but also let us take this*

only as a starting point: when someone talks, the other's responsibility is to hold that person accountable and safe. What could this look like? Arguing can be much more than just logically agreeing or contradicting each other. Let us be like children tirelessly asking "yes, but why?". Let us get carried away with enthusiasm, but also put some effort in questioning how things could be otherwise –there must be a myriad of alternatives, right? We can do something valuable. Let us be unashamed for a while, let us be curious and adventurous".

The choice of contributors followed a basic criteria set out by Flora Reznik, the curator of the event, in conversation with VHDG. The criteria read as follows: that each contributor's work is thoughtful, innovative, and valuable; that it resonates with the trigger-topic 'Unknown grounds'; that their practices are diverse, yet connectable (backgrounds varying from architecture to history, mathematics, philosophy, design, archival studies, and art); and that they work in The Netherlands yet come from all over the globe. The authors compiled in this publication rethink the possibilities of agency in relation to "unknown grounds." The texts are richly thought provoking as they oscillate between the abstract and the concrete. Each author is an interdisciplinary practitioner (the slash [/] is a crucial part of every contributor's biography), and each has developed distinctive approaches to address the initial prompt. With varying styles and concerns, the texts do not come together harmoniously, rather, they cohabit a space as a compilation, sometimes blissfully echoing each other, sometimes producing fruitful frictions.

Sissel Marie Tonn's "Daily Research" is a mix of poetic personal journaling and geological/artistic research, which served as a base to develop her artwork "The Intimate Earthquake Archive". This installation addresses the man-made earthquakes in the Dutch province of Groningen caused by the processes used to extract natural gas from the ground. Her work is attentive to sensory and perceptual structures of attention as well as perception within changing environments.

Andrej Radman is a theorist focusing on New Materialism, and the Ecologies of Architecture. "Groundless Grounds" is an example of a challenging specialized discourse, meaning a discourse that is humble yet courageous enough to dive into preceding texts. Not to use them as an authority, but to experiment with them like a chemist with a new compound. From the perspective of relational theory, he delves into an investigation of perception and the realm of affect, questioning the very notions of representation and communication. One statement in particular stands out: “one cannot understand a system unless one acts on it.”

Bert Looper’s background as a historian and archivist comes together with poetic sensitivity. “Unknown words, unknown grounds: Language, landscape and memory” invites us to consider the role of a language, specifically the Frisian language, in relation to landscape and memory. Far from nostalgic, a main question hovers over the whole text: How can language generate a ‘sense of place’ and environmental awareness, while acknowledging that an environment never ceases to change?

Theun Karelse’s ‘Machine Wilderness’ reflects on the history of landscape in European art and the emergence of landscapes in artificial minds. In his project ‘DeepSteward’, AI’s are left alone to learn from environments that have minimal human presence. His field research stems from the idea that: “the most urgent questions in our society are outside our front door, in what was previously called nature.” His project is hopeful and exciting, offering an alternative to the dark reality of AI learning from the worst of humanity.

masharu’s “Museum of Edible Earth” is a provocative artistic and sociological project that deals with personal desires while questioning the prejudices of public health institutions and so-called ‘common sense’. They research “Geophagy,” the practice of eating earth, not from a detached anthropological perspective, but one that is sincerely connected to the ground. A companion to their text, “Tasty, Edible Earth” by geologist Bert Boekschoten, depicts his personal and professional perspective on eating dirt.

Finally, Flora Reznik‘s contribution, “Of Asymmetrical Legs, Scars, Infrastructures and Exile,” is an exploration of how personal experience affects theoretical research, and vice versa. The text aims to provide a glimpse of the political-philosophical considerations that are embedded in her work, “Change on y, change on x,” a piece that re-imagines the scar on her brother’s leg as a fictive territory, playing with the multi-layered concept of trace. She aims to give ground (as unstable as it may be) to the possibility of new “strategic belongings”. A vulnerable notion of the self mingles with the old concept of political sovereignty and questions the distinction between a line that would separate the inside from the outside, from a jointure that keeps things connected.

Even though the texts generously shared by the contributors may not seem to directly address the issue of ‚open community‘ referred to in the Foreword in an explicit or concrete political sense, we would like to invite the reader to consider these approaches as each translating into their own specific field. In this sense, the political dimension of openness might not be so much ‘talked about’, but effectively performed. “Unknown Grounds” can function as a *worksite:* a small and incipient civil-political community that sets itself to the task of translation. In this case not necessarily linguistically speaking, but in terms of opening up the specific fields of inquiry, allowing passage from one to another whilst remaining attentive to the subtle connections between them.

---

1 This is the case for all of them except Ribal, who did not contribute a text, and for Bert Boekschoten, author of “Tasty, edible earth”, who did not participate in the performative symposium and therefore does not appear as a character in the “Script for a Synthetic Play”, yet he contributed a text, invited by masharu.

DAILY RESEARCH

SISSEL MARIE TONN

Does the meaning of the old peasants' proverb 'What you take from the land, you also have to put back' resonate with your contribution?

With the current climate crisis, what can embodiment (of time) add to another understanding of the future?

Are geological timescales that these samples reveal just too vast for us to comprehend? (As is often stated) Or do we just lack practice?

You feel mineral vibrations in your head when touching the stone. If the Burroughs quote "objects come alive with your life and will" is true, is the fact that they might also jump at you really a contradiction?

Is the tuning of our attention within an environment a voluntary act? Is it a political act?

What can we learn from rocks?

What is the difference between natural history and cultural history?

how is an artist bound by (or 'grounded' in) moral values, when dealing with a topic related to a situation where people suffer daily?

What kinds of rituals could we think of to make geological temporality accessible to our present?

How do we move with our environment?
What is holding us back/ what is pushing us forward?

How does your practice understand or relate to the notion of efficacy?

'How or in which way can we rethink language at its core in the light of human decentralization?'

What possibilities can we think of to collectivize engagement with the land, and what might we gain from that?

Are the earthquakes a form of protest from the earth? If so, a form of protest against what?

How do you reflect on your own role relating to this topic as an outsider (assuming you do not have any direct connections to Groningen)?

At first glance, the core sample suggests the appearance of meat on a butcher's block. An oddly shaped rock wrapped in tinfoil and twine, encapsulated in orange wax. It hides in the back of the storage shelves, in a dark corner of The Core Sample Storage Warehouse. No human hand has touched it for a long time, the layer of dust a testament to that fact. Moist pebbles are trapped within the skin-like waxy coating.

d concrete floor. My fingers run across the wax. I grab it firmly with my left hand and cling to it with hopeful intensity, probably akin to handling a talisman or some other magical object. I focus on the rock's hard surface in an attempt to regain my balance and fend off a burst of nausea that hit me just moments ago. I imagine its impenetrable insides and mentally conjure its steadiness for my own use. On the upper left side of my head I feel a hot vibration, like a trace left on the inside of my skull, shaped by the blow of a city bus mirror. It causes a strange itch, resembling the feeling of a phantom limb, — a place I am unable to scratch.

I practice becoming still as a rock. My limbs stiffen on the floor. I force my eyes still and freeze the movement of the images behind my eyelids, like a film coming to a clean stop amid a rolling motion. I picture one single monolithic core sample hovering in dark space. It is pristine, like "The Blue Marble," the last photo taken by human hands of the earth from space. This will help. I stop breathing and hear the blood raging past my eardrums. The tension straining my eyes slowly dissolves. I focus, once again, on a still point in the faded popcorn ceiling.

The same day I got hit by the city bus mirror, the neurologist asked me to walk in a straight line; to follow the movement of his fingers. Left to right. From centre to periphery. He pinched my arms and asked me to remember three things: a house, a tree, and a car. While lying on the hospital bed, the fear of forgetting those three words accumulated into a hard rock in my stomach. Something in my field of vision had shifted that day, as if the world transformed into a magic-eye image, where the hidden image can only be seen when the eyes lose focus.

The beginning of my interest in the man-made earthquakes in Groningen may have started while resting my concussed head on the cold concrete floor of The Core Sample Storage Warehouse, feeling the orange peel texture of the core sample's wax covering. Perhaps what caught my attention was its resemblance to an oversized pork chop, the wax's strange likeness to skin, and the heavy weight that made its appearance and consistency not quite add up. Or maybe it was later in the week, when I looked over the footage I shot that day of the rows upon rows of archived core samples, shaky and blurry, as if an internal earthquake affected my arms while shooting, as if this new strange blurring of my vision had infected the recording-instrument in my hand. The coincidence of encountering the phenomenon of man-made earthquakes at this moment of sensory disorientation seemed significant. I saw the earth's exhaustion as a larger narrative into which my own body's sensory exhaustion fit like a puzzle piece.

I am looking at a poster of geological periods in the office of The Core Sample Storage Warehouse. Here are the volcanoes that erupted in black masses of lava and consumed everything with their glowing tongues. Here are the ice sheets that molded the earth like modelling clay. Here, the forces of time that moved tectonic plates into slow and rapid collisions. Then the large bodies of water moved in. Then the sunlight evaporated the water and left a delicate icing of salt across the crust of the earth.

Man-made earthquakes? What a strange, poetic constellation of words. Writing poetically about this, however, is akin to the guilty pleasure of photographing oil spills for their colourful iridescent surface. I am aware.

The new chemistry of the air makes the rays of the sunset glow in unexpected ways. Peat reserves can burn underground throughout winter when the bog is hidden under a layer of ice. When the ice melts and a breath of oxygen reappears in the spring, the fire roars again. The shock of becoming geological has long worn off, or perhaps, it was never really there. The shock moved with the slowness of an ice sheet.

I set up an old canvas tent at the back of an isle of unused shelves, where I can spread out and do Daily Research.

DAILY RESEARCH (DR)

The process of firmly and rigorously taming the sensory exhaustion of perceiving the world as it unfolds. The nausea of looking at letters, screens, driving, biking, drawing, walking fast, talking at length to people, all of this requires the same kind of steady and slow discipline as that of taming a startled horse. One that did not sense the speed of the approaching bus, and now it snorts heavily with diluted nostrils and foam around the mouth.

DR is a scratching; a careful untangling of the threads of events interwoven through movement and vibration. When I become as still as a rock, I feel the difference recorded by my body, like fossilized traces of pre-historic critters on a sandstone surface. DR is a set of simple practices intended to keep track of these recordings. I am telling myself that the blow to my head of the city bus mirror benefits my research. It will help me become more attuned to the slow changes of the earth; it will help me record their significance.

A note is enclosed in the orange wax of the core sample states. The note reveals that it is Slochteren Sandstone, taken in the town of the same name in the 1950s. It carries deeply desirable information about the earth, of unexplored treasures hidden just below our feet. It embodies the triumphant incursion of earth's impenetrability. Perhaps, it was this very sample that determined the first drilling for gas in Slochteren, more than 60 years ago. As I hold the sample in my hand, I feel a subtle vibration. The tremors are soft, at the threshold of perception. These phantom vibrations make me wonder if my brain really is well. How much can you really discover without doing a brain scan? What if all objects start vibrating at my touch? I feel sweat drip down my spine. Then I remember a quote by William Burroughs, in the essay about the practice of Doing Easy — “Every object you touch is alive with your life and your will.” But elsewhere in the same essay he also states that “objects might jump out and stump against your toe or slam against your knuckle.” So, I guess, it's not so simple.

Before the companies started drilling into the earth, they took mile-long biopsies of the subsurface. These biopsies were meticulously examined by equipment so accurate that it could predict the day-to-day growth of a cancerous tumour. Each granule of sand was noted, and through a microscope they turned into fist-sized gems. When the right constellation of sedimentary rock was found, they cheered. Parliament passed a law that ordered The Core Sample Storage Warehouse to store all the samples collected in the country. They were brought to the warehouse in carefully wrapped plastic canisters, where they found their final resting place inside one of the layers of storage shelves. Some rocks are black with white arteries that glisten. Some are damp and dusty. Several are stored in mouldy wooden boxes. Salt cores leak with moisture, their brittle cloth enclosure perforated by crystals.

The keeper of The Core Sample Storage Warehouse handles the long cylindrical canisters with precision, but without particular affection. He has let me settle in the back of the long corridors, with an overbearing tolerance of my newfound obsession. Like a good archivist, he knows the shelves in the depths of the warehouse like the back of his hand, and patiently pulls out every mouldy wooden box that I desire. When he pulls the long boxes filled with resin-enclosed Limburg sandstone, his movements seem reduced to the bare minimum, but with ease, and a surprising strength for his small figure. I wonder if he vividly senses the dull presence of the rock samples too, and whether the loud talk radio is a way to mute their prattle. Apart from the daily management of the core samples coming in from the field, he is also in charge of an impressive collection of succulents and house plants, which inhabit the entrance area across from his glass cubicle. We stay largely uninterested in each other's research, hiding around the corners of the neatly organized storage shelves.

DAILY RESEARCH EXERCISE

I am moving along the rows of storage shelves at the far end of the left corridor in The Core Sample Storage Warehouse. My field of vision shoots like an arrow towards the deep dark at the end of the corridor. In rifle shooting it is called the fate line: the piercing, penetrating, deadly gaze. For this practice, a try wider, softer approach. I hold my index fingers at the periphery of each eye and shift my gaze outwards as much as possible. This peripheral vision exercise deconstructs the preconditioned sensory arrangements of my body. As I move deeper towards the darkness, I notice the rows of storage shelves moving with the waves of my gait. A slight shift of attention and the whole world animates with hidden movement. At the end of the rows, in the darkness, sits my orange tent. I keep records of these exercises in the margins of newspaper cut-outs:

After two unsuccessful attempts, the Slochteren 1 well drilled deeper and further. On 22 July 1959 they discovered a gas pocket in the Lower Permian sands, which proved worthy of commercial interest. There was little rejoicing — they had been looking for oil in the Upper Permian Zechstein. Only when two other drills also found large gas reservoirs, approximately at the same depth, they realized the significance of these discoveries, the huge 2.8 trillion cubic meter gas field in the porous Rotliegend formation spans from the United Kingdom across the Northern Sea to western Germany. From then on it was perceived that this was the discovery of a super-giant.

And just like that, 263-million-year-old material is forced into the present, reversing the speed with which tropical forest matter was folded into the Aeolian dunes in the Variscan age.

BURIAL HISTORY

Unlike human burials, which are often swift and procedural, the burial history of organic matter describes the ultra-slow folding process of decomposition into sedimentary layers. It is continuous across millennia, as the earth moves and overlaps, like dough being kneaded, over a span of time too great for the human mind to comprehend. As I move along the rows of storage shelves, noting them carefully through the corner of each eye, I imagine the entire warehouse as sediment, layers of knowledge of the subsurface of the country. The slowness of moving through the shelves brings forth new details of the archive: the texture of the light absorbed by dark wooden boxes or reflected by bright yellow storage units; the sharp smell of mould mixing with acrid resin.

Time seems lost inside the warehouse. Is it autumn? The keeper eyes my daily exercises with poorly hidden amusement while he goes about manually registering and archiving newly arrived core samples. Clearly, the smell of mouldy boxes does not make him dizzy. He shows me a large plastic tray, where different cut-outs of a long sample show the sedimentary layering of the subsurface in the Rotliegend Formation. The rocks are beautiful, like gemstones nestled into a shiny resin bed. He points at the pinkish sandy lumps of rock in the middle. “The best reservoirs for gas are found in the fine-grained Aeolian dune sands,” he says. “The rock formation where the gas is found today has desert origin, with sand dunes and wadis formed by rivers. The oscillation between wet and dry sands across millennia resulted in deposits of mudstones and halite.” His finger dances across the uneven dark lines that run through the rock, animating the material’s sharp cuts and soft waves.

“The rock records profound changes in climate, vegetation and sedimentary processes. Each core sample is a natural archive in itself,” he says. I picture Russian dolls; uncovering new shapes inside each other. Rock hard shells smashed with a pickaxe, to reveal another shimmering shell underneath; natural archives inside this large man-made archive that is The Core Sample Storage Warehouse. “It is possible to read the traces of time within the layers,” the keeper says. “Here the oceans rose and dried out again. This event left the layer of salt that acts as a seal for the gas, formed by the decomposing tropical vegetation in the sand dunes below. This is the awesome work time orchestrated for us to harvest the precious gasses now heating our houses and boiling our water.” His eyes are shining with the excitement of such specialized knowledge.

I picture gardens of prehistoric ferns and bushes with bright red berries decomposing as they are folded into an alien dune landscape. How they make space for themselves inside these folds, and how their exhales of methane gas mold pockets that press lightly against the salt layer of the Zechstein. These spans of time that are instrumental to geological formations are beyond human perception. The rock exposes these rhythms in comprehensible patterns of strata.

I recall a visit to a quarry in Germany in early autumn. My geologist friend pointed to the stripes along the wall of the quarry hovering above us. “Here changes in the tides are recorded! What this rock shows is the waxing and waning of the moon.” I was looking at the large drill holes into the rock. They hinted at the rock’s not-so distant future: It would eventually also be chopped into sizable blocks of sandstone used for staircases and courthouses. Dinosaur-sized digging machines stood dormant around a deep pit of green water, and the scent of decomposing leaves somehow made this millennial process slightly more tangible.

The Rotliegend Formation, better known as the Groningen Gas Field, has yielded earth gas since the 1950s. It whistles through long pipes perforating the salt layer shield of the Zechstein. Within a few years of the discovery, pipes grew out of the region and spread into the rest of the country, and soon after, across Europe and even North Africa. The gas not immediately used is pumped back into the natural reservoirs deep below the Zechstein seal, dormant until it is needed once again.

The speed that the ancient matter is excavated is orchestrated through the rapid developments of new extraction methods. The Groningen Gas Field is praised for the emergence of new revolutionizing methods for tapping the earth's resources with even greater efficiency, allocating the bounty, like pioneers tapping maple trees for syrup.

The keeper forms the shapes of gas reservoirs with his hands. Pulsating movements, like palpitating hearts, pushing air out from inside the palms. His usual demeanour of professional reserve seems somewhat deflated. His movements now emanate a tired precision, like that of a worn-out craftsman that has shaped hard metals for decades, or perhaps, a tarot reader that knows too much.

GROUNDLESS GROUNDS

ANDREJ RADMAN

Can doubt play a role in perceiving the ground we stand on, its solidness, its groundlessness?

If perception is a "skill" what are the potentials for it to be trained?

How does the ecological approach of perception relate to the performative and process-based character of current artistic practices?

How can architects and designers create space (ground) for freedom and subversion when neoliberal pressures push us in the opposite direction?

Is Radical Empiricism about beyond-human relations?

Where does the ground end?

How do you bring relational theory into practice in your work and everyday life?

Why should one widen the gap between perception and action?

What is an example of affordance and where can it be useful?

Can we perceive the virtual?

Isn't the artist or the architect always in search of the effect of the paradox 'Strange/familiar' in the perception of the work?

I like the statement: "one cannot understand a system unless one acts on it."

How could we adopt or develop a language that better facilitates a temporal, ecological approach?

The world does not speak to the observer. Animals and humans communicate with cries, gestures, speech, pictures, writing, and television [and internet], but we cannot hope to understand perception in terms of these channels; it is quite the other way around. Words and pictures convey information, carry it, or transmit it, but the information in the sea of energy around each of us, luminous or mechanical or chemical energy, is not conveyed. It is simply there. The assumption that information can be transmitted and the assumption that it can be stored are appropriate for the theory of communication, not for the theory of perception. (James J. Gibson).[1]

KINAESTHESIA

In his essay "Birth," Michel Serres recounts a dramatic story of a sailor whose vessel was on fire. In an attempt to escape out of a small window, he became trapped between the inferno of the burning cabin and the freezing cold of the rough seas. As he struggled to himself squeeze out, the sailor began to contemplate the sense of 'I.' At which point, he wondered, do I consider myself to be effectively outside; is it when the head alone is sticking out, or when the whole chest emerges, or . . .? This is a problem of coenaesthesia.[2]

Echoing Maurice Merleau-Ponty, Gregory Bateson goes even further (and I mean literally) in his *Steps to an Ecology of Mind*: "[C]onsider a blind man with a stick. Where does the blind man's self begin? At the tip of the stick? At the handle of the stick? Or at some point half-way up the stick?"[3] Kinaesthesia—which is even antecedent to coenaesthesia—is not *like* something, explains the champion of the Corporeal Turn, Maxine Sheets-Johnstone: it is what it is.[4] At around the same time (the early 1980s), Serres' compatriot Gilles Deleuze diagnoses the historical crisis of psychology: it was no longer attainable to place images in consciousness and movements in space.[5] Once the "ontological iron curtain" is raised, how is one to pass from one order to another?[6]

THE AFFECTIVE TURN

The Frenchmen did not seem aware of the parallel efforts by the American psychologist James Jerome Gibson, who published *The Ecological Approach to Visual Perception* in 1979. In what turned out to be his last book, Gibson set the course for a radical anti-representationalist approach to perception.[7] If we agree with Deleuze that filmmakers, painters, architects, and musicians are all essentially 'thinkers,' then the difference is that, unlike philosophers, they do not create concepts. They create 'percepts' (would-be perceptions) and 'affects' (capacities to affect and be affected). Gibson famously cautioned that it is a setback for architects to begin their training with a 'basic design' course because it was taught from an underlying assumption that understanding 'form' is as necessary for architects as it is, presumably, for painters. But, in his opinion, the use of the term 'form' only adds to the confusion. Instead, what architects ought to be concerned with are 'affordances'.[8] According to Gibson, it is safe to suggest that:

[M]en had not paid attention to the perspectives of things until they learned to draw and perceive by means of drawings. Before that time they needed only to detect the specifying invariants of things that differentiated

them—their distinctive features, not their momentary aspects or frozen projections. Young children are also . . . not aware of aspects of forms as such until they begin to notice pictures as surfaces.[9]

There is resonance between Gibson's ecological approach and Deleuze's theses from the first *Cinema* book. It is, however, unfortunate that in Deleuzian scholarship the 'Movement-Image' seems to be overshadowed by the subsequent volume dedicated to the 'Time-Image.'[10] Notwithstanding the theoretical capacity of the latter, the time is right — at least from the point of view of architectural discipline — to reopen the former. The Bergsonian trope 'Image = Movement' from *Cinema 1*, which might as well be attributed to Gibson, is yet to be unpacked.[11]

SPECULATIVE PRAGMATISM

Movement is a phenomenon *sui generis* that may detach itself from objects of sight. According to Gibson, neither signals nor pictures 'come through' the sense organs because they are components of perceptual *systems* that extract invariants from the stimulus energy flux that surrounds an observer. Invariants are specific to the world, but not to the receptors stimulated. Perception is therefore a skill, not a construction of the mental world out of psychic components. Information only needs to be detected; no mediation through memory, inferences or any other cognitive processes required.[12]

In his *Cinema* books, Deleuze relies heavily on Charles Sanders Peirce's 'three principles of Logic': Firstness, Secondness and Thirdness.[13] Peirce himself explains the triad as:

First is the conception of being or existing independent of anything else. Second is the conception of being relative to, the conception of reaction with, something else. Third is the conception of mediation, whereby a first and second are brought into relation . . . The origin of things, considered not as leading to anything, but in itself, contains the idea of First, the end of things that of Second, the process mediating between them that of Third.[14]

For Henri Bergson, there is also a 'degree zero' — *the plane of immanence* — from which signs take shape. Deleuze follows the lead of Bergson, for whom the image is more than what the idealist calls a 'representation' and less than what the realist calls a 'thing'. He thus identifies a dead end in the macro- and micro-reductionist approach of *rationalism* and *empiricism* respectively.[15] In the case of Gibson, the imperative was to navigate between exo-reductionist (quasi-materialist) *Behaviourism* and endo-reductionist (crypto-idealist) *Gestalt*.[16] The key is to go beyond the given (product), to that by which a given is given (process).[17] Let us for the sake of simplicity limit our inquiry to visual perception.

ICON: AMBIENT OPTIC ARRAY

Under the conventional theory, the starting point for perception is the retinal image. According to Gibson, however, the starting point is the 'Ambient Optic Array' that provides *direct* information about the media, surfaces, substances, and events for an observer. This 'compiled knowledge' is rich and reliable and not in need of mediating processes. The optical structure is generated by the layout of surfaces. It is potentially, and not necessarily effectively, available for perception. Each edge and surface projects a unique and specific pattern of optical discontinuities to each *potential* point of view. The concept of 'Ambient Optic Array' could fall under Peirce's Firstness.

INDEX: OPTICAL FLOW FIELD

Gibson's concept of 'Optical Flow Field' falls under Peirce's Secondness. The Optical Flow Field results from the locomotion of an organism in a cluttered environment. When an organism moves forward there is a global transformation of the solid angle that produces a vectorial movement of each optical texture. The law of optical expansion (looming) gives a basis for goal-directed movement: "To start moving, make the optic array flow. To stop, cancel the flow. To go back, make the flow reverse."[18]

SYMBOL: AFFORDANCE

Finally, Thirdness is the mode of being, which brings interaction into relationship with a context of constraint (quasi-cause) akin to Gibson's concept of Affordances (e.g., walk-through-ability). Traditionally, a shape has to be visually perceived through two instantaneous values: static retinal form (image) and the momentary distance value of depth cues (inference). But the affordance perceived is *not based on a static property such as form, but rather upon an invariant embedded in change* (hence the title of the paper — "Groundless Grounds").

The concept of the invariant, as a figure of time (and not space), might prove indispensable for answering difficult questions such as: What is the ontological status of looming and locomoting as the *relata* of the 'ecological law', i.e., the *relation* that is exterior to its terms? It is this sort of ontological question that the ecological approach addresses. Before we deal with them let us dwell a little longer on some contemporary realist speculations.[19]

ABDUCTION

In his contribution to the *Speculations on Anonymous Materials* Symposium, Reza Negarestani underscored Peircean abduction as a form of 'material inference.' In contrast to classical, i.e., formal logic, abduction is fallible given that information is gathered by way of manipulation. His case is straightforward: one cannot understand a system unless one acts on it. The behaviour of a system is, in turn, dependent on the concept of tendencies, which cannot be intuited unless one is to intervene in the causal fabric (by locomotion in the case of perception).

Another term for such a device of manipulation is *heuristics*, neither deductive nor inductive, but *material* inference. It is material in the sense that it is non-formal, as it does not abide by logical norms. It preserves neither foundation, nor truth. The problem of non-entailment is overcome by turning the system into a 'living hypothesis'. As with our threefold example, to render anything intelligible, the scope of manipulation needs to be deepened. The 'constructability' then becomes isomorphic with the understanding of what this or that is, or better, what it affords (what its affects are). In the words of Negarestani:

Heuristics are not analytical devices. They are synthetic operators. They treat material as a problem. But they don't break this problem into pieces. They transform this problem into a new problem. And this is what the preservation of invariance is...the problem now can be approached and solved on a simpler, more optimal level. Hence, the understanding that the system is nothing but its behaviour and behaviour is a register of constructability.[20]

RADICAL EMPIRICISM

A healthy dose of scepticism led Gibson to conclude that the perplexing lack of correlation between proximal stimulation and perception is due to the mere arbitrariness of physical dimensions of the stimulus.[21] This, in turn, led him to a further conclusion that the appropriate level of describing perception is *ecology*, and not physics or geometry, as adopted in the conventional theory of perception. "Perception has no object" is an assertion by Deleuze, which might as well be attributed to Gibson.[22] It is "hallucinatory" because it has no object and presupposes no object, because it has not yet been constituted (constructed). There is then, of course, no (fully constituted) subject either.

The ecological ontology, which Gibson developed to displace Cartesian dualism, is therefore circumscribed by invariant relations or patterns of becoming that need to be defined relative to an appropriate domain of validity. This *direct* perception is based on the ecological realist position, which takes things to appear as they *do* because that is the way they *are*, as taken in reference to the *acting* perceiver at the ecological (meso)scale. The stance is not to be confused with naïve realism that is absolute, where things appear exactly as they are and unconditionally so. As William James defined it, there are five guidelines of radical empiricism. In the words of Brian Massumi:

Everything that is, is in perception. (Please note that the first guideline also applies to classical empiricism; radical empiricism begins to part company with classical empiricism in the second guideline).

Take everything as it comes. You cannot pick and choose according to priori principles or pre-given evaluative criteria.

Relations must be accounted as being as real as the terms related. In other words, relations have a mode of reality distinct from that of the discrete objects we find in relation.

Relations are not only real, they are *really* perceived, and directly so. Relations not only have their own mode of reality, but each has its own immediate mode of appearance [e.g., looming].

"Ninety-nine times out of a hundred" the terms and relations that appear "are not actually, but only virtually there."[23]

Our engaged understanding of the world is based not on simulation or matching what we see, but on enactive perceptual and interactive processes. Steven Shaviro explains a kindred contribution to the enactive approach to cognition by the process philosopher Alfred North Whitehead:

Western philosophy since Descartes gives far too large a place to "presentational immediacy," or the clear and distinct representation of sensations in the mind of a conscious, perceiving subject. In fact, such perception is far less common, and far less important than what Whitehead calls "perception in the mode of causal efficacy," or the "vague" (nonrepresentational) way that entities affect and are affected by one another through a process of vector transmission. Presentational immediacy does not merit the transcendental or constitutive role that Kant attributes to it. For this mode of perception is confined to "high-grade organisms" that are "relatively few" in the universe as a whole. On the other hand, causal efficacy is universal; it plays a larger role in our own experience than we tend to realize, and it can be attributed 'even to organisms of the lowest grade'.[24]

INSERTING THE INTERVAL

Representational theories of perception postulate an isolated and autonomous subject; set apart from its milieu, it is utterly dependent on the process of mental representation.

Furthermore, this process is often staged for another interiorized subject. Gibson repeatedly cautioned against the homunculus thesis, "The movements of the hands do not consist of responses to stimuli. . . This is surely an error. The alternative is not a return to mentalism. We should think of the hands as neither triggered nor commanded but controlled."[25] As Massumi puts it, a "zone of indeterminacy" is glimpsed in the hyphen between the stimulus and response (S-R): "Thought consists in widening that gap, filling it fuller and fuller with potential responses."[26] The task of the architect, as I see it, is to widen the gap between perception and action. For what is *affordance* (Gibson's neologism for 'would-be action') if not the hyphen between the two? In opposition to a deterministic schema of perception leading to a certain action, affordance is always relational, that is, non-deterministic. Here is the definition by Gibson himself:

An important fact about affordances of the environment is that they are in a sense objective, real, and physical, unlike values and meanings, which are often supposed to be subjective, phenomenal, and mental. Yet, actually, an affordance is neither an objective nor a subjective property; or it is both if you like. An affordance cuts across the dichotomy of subjective-objective and helps us to understand its inadequacy. It is both physical and psychical, yet neither. An affordance points both ways, to the environment and to the observer.[27]

CONCLUSION

Unfortunately, a great deal of the artificial intelligence research that has direct influence on contemporary architectural discourse continues to be based on template-matching strategies, making Karl Popper's famous metaphor of the 'bucket theory of mind' difficult to dispense.[28] Unwittingly, it perpetuates the Platonic division between visible appearances and intelligible essences.

By way of conclusion, let us briefly remind ourselves of what constitutes the pernicious representational view. In order for a life form to perceive X, it relies on the concept of X. Furthermore, if 'inputs' require concepts to be meaningful, then concepts must precede 'inputs,' as in *nativism*. Conversely, if concepts require 'input' for their content, then 'inputs' must precede concepts, as in *empiricism*. A hopeful way out of this deadlock might be to consider a different form of 'universality,' one that is no longer grounded on *commonality.*

Representational view is a misleading term. What if drawing is not copying, if it is impossible to copy (or re-present) a piece of environment? What if information is unlimited and the concept of projection is useless; all from the point of view of perception? Ignorance is no defence. We are in need of a critique of the conception of the world as an optical phenomenon.[29] Our all-too-ocular centric theories require major updating.[30] According to Gregory Flaxman, the image is neither a representation of an object nor a visual impression, the first of which connotes mere re-cognition and the second a limited sensory bandwidth. Rather, the image is a collection of sensations — a 'sensible aggregate,' or what Deleuze will ultimately call a 'sign.' As Deleuze himself explains, "The movement-image is the modulation of the object itself."[31]

Curiously enough, the *ambulatory* dimension of vision seems to have eluded the greatest of authorities in the field.[32] Architects are known to be keen readers of the Sci-Fi writer William Gibson.[33] However, if we are to unlock the real virtuality, rather than the crypto-Cartesian virtual reality, another Gibson is in order. I will conclude with his caveat, which seems timelier than ever: "Being intellectually lazy, we try to understand perception in the same way we understand communication, in terms of the familiar."[34]

UNKNOWN WORDS, UNKNOWN GROUNDS

Language, landscape, and memory

BERT LOOPER

Will Frisian still be a “language of memory” when its speakers take off their Arcadian goggles?

In what way could we let the ground talk (back) to us?

Where and how in popular and/or street culture does language already play a role in shaping our sense of place?

Is language a tool for access to an environment?

Could you imagine Frisian becoming a "language of imagination" instead of "fossilised language"

Could there be a sci–fi Frisian?

As an archivist, would you say that the collective imaginary has infinite space or are the 'shelves' of memory limited?

How can we go beyond preaching to the choir?

Should we use the words of yesterday or make the words of tomorrow?

If a common ground is related to language, can there be common ground among different nations?

Can we use language to cross borders, or does it create borders? How to make a language breathe?

How to shape the new with old words?

Not everyone will be as affected as philosopher Ton Lemaire, but many of us will be able to identify with the way Lemaire describes the feeling of losing 'animated places', in fact, 'losing grounds'. In *Met open zinnen* (With open sentences, from 2002) Lemaire states: "Although we are prepared to measure and face the ecological impoverishment (...) hardly anyone has an eye for the psychological damage that people can suffer from radical changes in their environment (...) As far as I am concerned: many landscapes that I had in my youth have changed since then. Every time such a dear place was mutilated, a piece of my youth was taken away from me because my soul was fused with the soul of the landscape." Lemaire makes clear that the relationship between man and landscape is intense and intimate. But in this relationship, there is always a third in the game: language. Because we are in Fryslân and because, for many of us, Fryslân is 'unknown grounds', I would like to focus on these 'grounds' to elaborate on the complex triangular relationship that is landscape–language–memory.

I would like to call Frisian the language of memory. Our language is overloaded with words and expressions that were once connected with a direct reality, but now only evokes images and memories of a sunken world. Of course, Dutch and English are also filled with images and style figures that are no longer connected to reality, but I would dare to say that Frisian poetry has become fossilised. In fact, I have noticed that when a Frisian speaker punctuates their arguments with as many old sayings and archaisms as possible, they are received very positively. We call that 'geef Frysk' (pure Frisian), but it contains an increasing number of words that have lost their meaning.

Currently, Frisian culture is shifting from the domain of language and history and towards that of experience. In doing so, language itself is losing ground in the domain of knowledge and is shifting towards the world of experience. Language is increasingly seen as part of the "Fryslân experience" and that process is accompanied by the archaization of the language, the more exotic Frisian, the stronger the experience. This development is not only caused by the power of the experience industry, but also because Frisians, as previously stated, assign many normative values to the archaic, for the sake of 'geef Frysk'. Accordingly, a self-reinforcing process is created. Folklorization makes it impossible for language to be the bearer of research, experiment, and innovation. Language stagnation is no longer an instrument for naming and searching for the future, but for preserving the past. Frisian is the language of memory: words and expressions hold the collective memory of an idyllic agricultural culture. Those words and expressions still have meaning for the older generations because they are within their memories, but for younger generations, the language becomes a museum.

I grew up in Friesland in the 1960s, and yet did not discover rich Frisian literature until the 1980s. This discovery was made through encountering Obe Postma's poetry, in particular his poems about the Frisian countryside of the early twentieth century. A writing style that had direct poetic power. His poetry gave me access to the same, still meaningful reality of the sixties, to well-known grounds: *'waarom is it bûthús'*, *'wyt en gielbûnt de âlde finne'*, *'de skries ropt en heech stiet de ljurk'*, *'by skerne en dobbe, dêr komt in fine rook no wei'*. For me, these words intensively and intimately forge language, landscape, and memory together. For younger generations, the poems of Postma no longer depict a known world because the poetic reality is no longer recognizable. Here, we touch upon the dilemma of the "bûthús" and the "âlde finne." We cannot restore the poetic reality of the comfortable cowshed and the beautiful colours of the meadow to give these words meaning once again. We cannot expect new generations to be inspired by an archaic and folkloric language.

The Frisian language is in a dire and defensive position, but perhaps, there is a way out. Not through legislation, European charter, or enforced obligation, but through re-centring the power of language and connecting language and landscape. Power does not lie in the use of what we call 'pure Frysk', the words and expressions that want to be as far away as possible from reality. The power of the Frisian language is in its ability to stimulate our 'sense of place' (spatial awareness). 'Sense of place' is also of great importance for new generations because it is about the relationship between the landscape and the human heart.

In Robert Macfarlane's recently published book, *Landmarks,* the main concern is the "power of language to shape our sense of place" (the power of language to form spatial awareness). Macfarlane describes how many words concerning nature have been deleted in the new edition of the *Oxford Junior Dictionary*. The missing words include willow, heather, lark, fern, and meadow. Yet at the same time, many new words have been introduced: voicemail, blog, broadband, and so on. In the 'dictionary', the outdoors and the natural are out of place in relation to the indoors and the virtual. The latter two concepts are, of course, aspects of a new sense of place, but it is crucial here that an existing reality is no longer named. Heather, ferns, and willows are still growing, but the landscape is no longer growing *with* language and therefore no longer produces tangible images and memories.

In his book, Macfarlane wants to aid both the language and the landscape. He collected thousands of words from various British regions to show how language not only describes reality but is also a means to know and love the landscape more intimately. Sometimes, the magic of old words is so great that their meaning is revived; connected again with reality and given access to memories. But that requires a very active, investigative approach to language. Macfarlane holds a mirror in front of us to guard language against the dangers of "fetishizing dialect and archaism".

When I read a famous Old Frisian Medieval legal text that described a fatherless child, I was struck by the passage that described how a child lacked their father's protection against hunger and the "niwelkalda winter". The spark! The magic of that word. A deepening relationship with nature. Oebele Vries translates the "niwelkalda winter" into Dutch as "the cold winter mist," but how much stronger and more beautiful is the translation 'diiskâlde winter'. I use the word 'diiskâld' often. It is more beautiful than cold water, and it is simply more apt to use 'diiskâld' (fog cold) rather than 'iiskâld' (ice cold). Yet, I could not find 'diiskâld' in the dictionary, though it is such a powerful word from the raw medieval Frisian reality that enriches our perception of nature and landscape.

The richness of other languages is often pointed out. The Eskimos, for example, have numerous words for snow. But do not forget that Frisians also have many names for numerous kinds of wind, mist, and rain. In *The History of Countryside* (1986), botanist Oliver Rackham describes four ways in which the landscape disappears: through loss of beauty (impoverishment), loss of freedom (fences, prohibition signs and gated festivals), loss of flora and fauna, and loss of meaning. The final example is the most difficult to measure, Macfarlane writes, that it would be fantastic if we actively developed a vocabulary that enriches life, stimulates imagination, and establishes creative relationships between people, and, additionally, between people and nature and landscape. That one word 'diiskâld' had all that effect, thanks to the old Frisians.

We lose the old landscape, but with old 'landscape-language' we try to ease the pain. However, the result is that we also risk losing the language altogether. The discrepancy between words, images, style figures, and reality becomes too large. The language loses meaning. We can turn the tide by actively using our language to investigate the current reality. That also means that we must see reality and find words for our descriptions. A relevant example is *Poisonous Summer,* a project that followed the construction of the waste incinerator in Harlingen. Writers, poets, and artists sought new words and images to shape their relationship with the polluted landscape. Language and landscape became connected in an honest way again. The aesthetic space, which was always the Frisian landscape, now also became a committed space. *Poisonous Summer* shows a fundamental shift in our sense of space and landscape. The strong mythical tradition in Frisian landscape poetry created a tension between the literary landscape of the past and the landscape of the present. The myth wanted to make the landscape unchangeable, but the interconnected realities of meadows without birds, industrial fishing on the tidal flats, the construction of roads, gas drilling, and waste ovens continue.

Obe Postma's literary landscapes are in our heads, and we no longer see the impoverishment of the current landscape through those same lenses. Because of its poetic tradition, Fryslân has become the land of memory, so much so that we still want to see the colours of the "finne" (meadow) even in the monotonous ryegrass lands. In *Poisonous Summer,* the magic of mythical poetry was broken, and the current landscape made its entrance into Frisian art and literature. The poets have taken off their Arcadian glasses and returned to an engagement with landscape in their work. From this renewed commitment, language and art, again, become the tools to relate to a rapidly changing landscape. We create a modern "sense of place" with the beautiful and new developments in the landscape. The triangular relationship between language, landscape, and memory still has every opportunity to become exciting and vital again. It is important that Frisian be given the space and attention to become, perhaps stumbling and groping, the language that investigates current and future events. That is a great opportunity but also a challenge.

When are we going to experience the actualization of these possibilities? Are we ready to face the challenges that will get us there? The Frisian literary world is not yet critically concerned with the question of what long term effects Cultural Capital 2018 will have for the position and development of literature and language. It is not entirely clear what Cultural Capital has delivered for the Frisian language and culture. Will our language and culture play a merely supportive role, or will it be central to the story we want to tell Europe. The relationship between language, landscape, and memory is a current and urgent European theme. Through language and literature, specifically Frisian language and literature, we can show the power of language to shape our sense of place.

MACHINE WILDERNESS

THEUN KARELSE

How can we hold machines (or rather the operations we ask them to perform) accountable if their workings become opaque?

Are you willing to surrender responsibility/accountability in design?

Can the trace of the human be totally erased in AI?

Assuming that automated learning software will adapt our language and find ways to eliminate its ambiguity and misapprehensions: in which ways will this affect political communication and interpersonal relationships?

If we lose the ability to understand/communicate with our machines, are we going to become irrelevant to them?

How can multi-species design methodologies truly move beyond human-centred design?

Could we perceive Machines as the ideal agents, these radical non-isolated participants, that may be captured by the term 'otherness'?

Can artificial intelligence overcome the human view on its surroundings?

When landscape first appeared as a subject in European art, it emerged as a landscape of symbols. The features that populated Gothic depictions of Earth served primarily as convenient symbols that formed a narrative. Some natural objects were treated realistically, but many – like the fantastical mountain formations depicted in *Thebaid*[1] – were almost ideograms for mountains taken straight from Byzantine tradition. This is a landscape seen over the shoulders of the main subject: humans (patrons) and biblical figures. A space where features are tagged placeholders in a larger narrative geography.

According to eminent art historian Kenneth Clarck, for Flemish painter Jan van Eyck, the environment first appeared as a landscape of fact. "In a single lifetime", Clarck writes in *Landscape into Art*[*], "van Eyck progressed the history of art in a way that an unsuspecting art historian might assume to take centuries. In these first 'modern' landscapes, van Eyck achieves by color, a tone of light that seems to already fully breathe the air of the Renaissance."

At present, landscape is emerging in artificial minds through machine learning from domains of precision such as agriculture, mining, forestry, autonomous vehicle navigation and ecology. Until recently, the ability to make sense of the environment was limited to biological beings, but machines are now blurring those lines. I'm interested in shifting the debate centred on machine intelligence beyond human-centred preoccupations – like job security, privacy, and politics — and towards the impact of these technologies on non-human lives, i.e., the other 99.99% of life on Earth.

THE MACHINE GAZE

From machine perception, the environment seems to emerge as a landscape of commodity. Unlike the painting tradition, machine perceptions of landscape aren't rooted in Byzantine art, but defined by platforms and training sets that humans provide. Leading image classifier platforms like *Inception* typically include household items, human infrastructure, and machinery, but also a peculiar collection of animal and plant species, such as, for instance, hundreds of dog breeds. These organisms do not refer to any existing ecosystem but are handpicked according to the interests of humans. When such an AI is introduced to a real-world terrain, these pre-trained sets prove about as relevant as cat-videos to the work of a marine-ecologist. For example, during our Ars Bioarctica residency in the Finnish Arctic in 2018, we turned the camera-eye to the surroundings of the Kilpisjarvi Biological Research Station where the machine gazed across a snow-covered terrain. Our human eyes saw hundreds of birch trees, lichen-covered rocks and perhaps some passing birds, but when asked, the AI said it only saw snowmobiles. There were none. It was hallucinating. It was hallucinating a landscape full of snowmobiles. And perhaps even more strikingly, it didn't see the trees.

The worldview of these platform A.I.s is largely populated by human artefacts, including snowmobiles, vacuum cleaners, and even guillotines. Like us, the worldview of our technology isn't neutral. Our landscapes, however, are still full of trees before they are planks; rocks before they are architecture; water before it is Evian. As it turns out cyborgs do not dream of electric sheep but have much more commodity-centred imaginations. Platform A.I.s of late capitalism develop as human centred. With much of the world's current environmental predicament stemming from anthropocentric bias, a number of questions are therefore raised: is it problematic that machines learn exclusively from humans? Is it problematic that their current habitat is corporate? Do intelligent machines need training-forests, like the ones for orphaned orangutans in rehabilitation programmes? Do the artificial agents that are currently taking seats in corporate boardrooms need to spend their weekends floating around coral reefs, volunteering at organic farms, or wandering the tundra among reindeer? Should machines also learn directly from animals and plants? If a machine is less confined to human classifications, would it invent something radically different from Linnaean taxonomy? What features of natural phenomena would catch its attention and into what kinds of unknown bestiaries would it cluster them?

DEEPSTEWARD

In an experimental set-up called DeepSteward, currently at Het Nieuwe Instituut in Rotterdam, Ian Ingram and I are exploring these questions. While an artificial agent oversees the large pond at HNI, we are tasked with determining how the machine could be given more freedom to interpret the natural world. The first results show, for instance, how the clusters that the machine makes are sometimes impossible for humans to decipher. They can be extremely similar looking. Although we're currently working primarily with images, we intend to radically broaden the scope for learning. This is in line with our more general impression that building a machine that looks at the world has forced us to reflect quite deeply on our own human perceptions. The complete naivety of the artificial agent confronts all the perceptual steps we take for granted, somewhat reminiscent of the experiences of British neurologist Dr. Oliver Sacks when confronted with patients suffering from very specific neurological damage.

DeepSteward developed from a broader exploration into environmental machine learning called Random Forests. This was a one-year research program based on fieldwork sessions with selected teams in locations that related to specific research questions. In turn, this research stemmed from a longer research project with a similar approach called Machine Wilderness, which challenged the convention of perceiving machines as assets of the human domain (in the sense that the biosphere and technosphere do not exist as separate realms). This may seem obvious, but it's hard to find an example of technology that is inclusive of all life. After centuries of designing infrastructure only for humans (and domesticated animals), we are gradually stepping into multi-species design methodologies. Of course, this is because the industrial revolution has decimated other organisms to a level where entire ecosystems are collapsing, but also because it is mind-numbingly boring to include only one specific species of ape.

FIELDWORK

We live in an increasingly unstable, rapidly changing world. As a result, we are constantly moving into unknown grounds. The programs described here are set in the middle of this dynamic, because we think and act differently in the presence of other beings, whilst in natural flows or in the middle of a sandstorm, and like us, our machines and algorithms need to be contaminated by other kinds of life.

I'll conclude by stating my perception: fieldwork is a crucial ingredient to artistic practice. Fieldwork isn't just *being outside,* as stated by eminent landscape thinker Jan de Graaf, but is a method of enquiry that starts from radical non-isolation of participants: perceiving, being and working in full exposure to the complexities and subtleties of an environment; navigating in collaboration with local experts, including artistic or scientific researchers, indigenous tribes, or semi-traditional hunter/gatherers. Fieldwork is a multi-sensory exploration based on direct experience, open-ended experimentation and in-situ prototyping that starts from local circumstances, complexities, and relations. Enquiry is an embodied act that seeks, in the words of Jens Hauser, to be "un-split" from environmental processes, natural cycles, climatic conditions, seasons, (non)human cultures; and, collectively, may be captured by the term 'otherness'. To work among other humans, other species, non-biological agents, and algorithms is exposing. Among others we can expand our faculties and more fully engage with unknown territory.

1 The term Thebaid refers to the representation of a rocky landscape in which a group of monks are engaged in various activities related to their life of prayer and asceticism. The term derived from a collection of texts recounting the lives of the saints in the desert, which told of the monks who in the first centuries of Christianity would withdraw to the desert around the Egyptian city of Thebes to pray and live as ascetics. This theme was particularly popular in Florence in the fifteenth century when it was depicted on rectangular panels, and this painting in the Uffizi is the only fully intact example still in existence today. In the landscape, numerous scenes from the legendary lives of various saints, including Saint Onuphrius and Saint Anthony, are alternated with scenes of daily life - the saint drawing water from the well, the saint riding a deer and the group carrying an elder on a stretcher, for example - which outline the monks' path to ascension. The luxuriant landscape is dominated by a river flowing into the sea and is filled with trees, a metaphor of the spiritual garden where the virtuous ascetics would prosper.

The painting conveys a strong sense of spirituality, and the origins of these figurations can be found in the enlightened environment of Florentine monasticism; however, they were also greatly appreciated by laypeople and indeed the Medici family owned two such examples. The painting exhibited at the Uffizi is thought to be the work of the Dominican friar Fra Angelico, but this attribution is not universally accepted.

MUSEUM OF EDIBLE EARTH

MASHARU

If we only have experience of the concrete, the singular, how can one access a realm of the universal, the spiritual?

What is it to connect with an environment?

Would the actual tasting experience change my attitude towards the idea of it?

Is this activity primarily about pleasure? What do we find so terrifying in our culture about unsanctioned, dirt-y acts of pleasure?

How can we explain that industrial societies hold earth and dirt in contempt and what does this say about their culture?

If you can make your own composition of soil, can you compose your origin too?

How important is sharing geophagy through eating earth together?

Do you make the earth yours, with all its history and culture, by eating it?

How does a body feel at home and how does a mind settle to a place?

Would you consider consuming non-terrestrial soils?

"She went back to eating earth... she persevered, overcome by the growing anxiety, and little by little she was getting back her ancestral appetite, the taste of primary minerals, the unbridled satisfaction of what was the original food. She would put handfuls of earth in her pockets, and ate them in small bits without being seen, with a confused feeling of pleasure..."
—Gabriel García Márquez, One Hundred Years of Solitude

Eating earth has been present in my artistic practice since 2011. In my performances and installations, I invite the audience to taste various types of soils and ceramics. During 'Unknown Grounds' I wanted to share my creative practice, which is, just as much, my personal practice. It is up to you if you want to take it or not. Please, be aware that EATING EARTH IS NOT RECOMMENDED BY THE FOOD AUTHORITY (ESPECIALLY FOR PREGNANT WOMEN) AND IS AT YOUR OWN RISK.

I always wanted to eat earth. This project is the realization of my desires.

The text below (particularly the last two paragraphs) was partly developed for the performance 'Surpassing the Beeline', directed by Abhishek Thapar in 2018

Since childhood, I have wanted to eat earth. On the playground, I ate sand. But after I grew up, I found the earth to not be such a socially acceptable food. I didn't dare to taste it again, until I moved to the Netherlands. At Eindhoven University of Technology, I started to secretly eat school board chalk, which is an earth-like substance. The taste was amazing, but it had a strange, artificial aftertaste of shampoo or washing-up liquid which made me feel very unwell. But the pure chalk taste – I wanted more and more of it, an unexplainable desire. I went to a health shop and asked for edible earth, and found that indeed, it does exist on the Dutch market, but was sold out in that particular shop. The clerk recommended a clay facemask, explaining that they themselves were eating it to clean the body from the inside and obtain the material's minerals. I sought more information online.

On the Internet, a Dutch health and alternative medicine activist wrote about the facemask that I purchased: „Green clay is a living, intelligent substance with an exceptional character. The package says: 'For external use only' because the European Union takes care to withdraw all healing remedies from the market. But eat it! It's good for you". On Wikipedia, I found that according to the DSM (Diagnostic and Statistical Manual of Mental Disorders, published by American Psychiatric Association) eating earth can be connected to a psychological disorder (pica), which is associated with development disabilities, such as autism, maternal deprivation, family issues, parental neglect, and disorganized family structures. On Dutch forums, I read that freaks and immigrants mostly eat earth.

In 2014, the Dutch Food Authority conducted a research study into edible clay available on the Dutch market. More than 60 types of edible earth were tested, some of which included toxic elements, such as arsenic and lead. None of the types originated from Dutch ground, and they were mostly consumed by immigrants and minority-cultural communities. As a result of this research, a few shops received fines for selling edible earth.

After 11 years of living in the Netherlands, I still do not feel completely Dutch. I will always be an immigrant. At the same time, I do not feel Russian anymore, still asking myself, who am I? I went back to Russia to eat white chalk from the sacred mountains where orthodox churches and monasteries are located. Because of the religion, I had to wear a long skirt and a headscarf to enter these territories. I really desired that chalk, and even though it seemed pure and sourced directly from nature, I was getting stomach pain, but I couldn't stop eating it.

For the past year, I have been in the practice of collecting and eating earth from across the world. Sometimes, it makes me feel like a world citizen. I started mixing different types of edible earth from different countries. This material has memory and keeps history of what the land has experienced. To make sense of who I am, I listened to these materials. From listening, I discovered it had experienced shifting homes, wind, turbulences, love, loss. It would inform me rather than I inform it. Earth knows better than I do. I wanted to map the right composition of the material, which would sustain, and could represent me. However, different types of clay repel each other, and remain fluid. Of course, I still take pieces and eat them.

BACKGROUND

"Soils significantly influence a variety of functions [...] that sustains the human population. Through ingestion (either deliberate or involuntary), inhalation and dermal absorption, the mineral, chemical and biological components of soils can either be directly beneficial or detrimental to human health."

Geophagy is the act of eating soil and soil-like substances, such as clay and chalk. Eating earth is an ancient spiritual and healing practice. It is still part of the cultures of a number of countries across the globe. For example, in Ghana, Guatemala, Indonesia, Kazakhstan, Kyrgyzstan, Nigeria, Suriname, Uzbekistan, and other countries across Africa, Asia and South America, clay is sold as an edible product on the market. Conversely, in the United States and Europe, geophagy is regarded as a psychological disorder and is included into the DSM-V. However, some people in the Netherlands still practice various types of earth eating. A number of popular brands available in 'health' shops (such as Ecoplaza and Biomarkt) provide soil specifically for ingestion. A select number of clays from Tanzania, Nigeria, Ghana, and Suriname are available on the Dutch market, although most are unlabelled.

Geophagy among animals as well as among humans is scientifically researched. Papers on the subject have been published in journals on anthropology, history, psychology, sociology, chemistry, and biology. The perception of earth in different cultures varies. Regardless of a strong connection to the land, nowadays industrialized societies do not hold earth in high esteem. In American English, expressions such as "dirty," "dirt poor," "dirt cheap," and "dirt bag" refer to undesirable things or people, as do other earth-related terms, "soiled," "muddy," "mudslinging," and "muck." If the "salt of the earth" is the best, the worst food "tastes like dirt." In addition, phrases like "dirt-poor," "soiled," "old as dirt," and "dirty minded" are also widespread." ;

When searching 'eating clay' on the Internet, developing countries are subjects of most of the hits. Notably, it is an old European and, in particular, Dutch tradition (edible holy earth is still available nowadays at St. Gerlachuskerk in Houthem near Limburg). Yet despite this, the Dutch Food Authority suggests that the oral use of clay should be discouraged since its toxicity can seriously damage health. Various communities in the Netherlands neglect these warnings.

In her book, *Religious Geophagy: Sacredness You Can Swallow*, Sera Young emphasizes that religiously prescribed geophagy in Christianity, Islam, Hinduism and Hoodoo is exempt from 'dirty connotations'. The same is true for geophagy as a part of a cultural pattern, as described in the DSM-V. In her earlier studies, Young raises the question of predominantly negative perceptions of geophagy, and the difficulties of being "aware of the ways in which geophagia may affect the body that fall outside of our respective disciplines." There is a viewpoint that because of the breakthroughs in medicine and advanced knowledge, we are culturally unable to understand the possible benefits and potential negative consequences of eating earth.

MUSEUM OF EDIBLE EARTH

With the goal to understand the reality of contemporary geophagy, and to also constitute a research base for the Museum of Edible Earth, the masharu studio has been building an extensive database of edible soils for oral consumption available on the market. More than 400 different soils from 35 countries have been purchased through the Internet, in cultural shops, as well as being obtained during field trips, to form the foundation of the Museum of Edible Earth.

The Museum of Edible Earth brings together a collection of edible soils from across the globe, inviting audiences to creatively review their knowledge about food and cultural traditions. The Museum of Edible Earth addresses the following questions: What stands behind earth-eating traditions? Where does edible earth come from? What are the possible benefits and dangers of eating earth? How do the material properties of earth affect flavour? The Museum's goal is to constitute an extensive collection of soils suggested for oral consumption from as many countries as possible and to catalogue their cultural uses and histories, but also to redesign and reconsider earth through cross-disciplinary partnerships, workshops, and collaborations.

The project Museum of Edible Earth has been developed with support of Creative Industries Fund NL, NIAS-KNAW, Akademie van Kunsten, Satellietgroep and Amsterdams Fonds Voor De Kunst. The masharu studio team that worked on the project are: masharu, Irene Kobalchuk, SasaHara, Ielyj Ivgi and Jester Van schuylenburch. Graphic design is by Olga Ganzha.

TASTY, EDIBLE EARTH

BERT BOEKSCHOTEN

I am a geologist — the earth is my business. As a soil science student, I remember tasting soil as a formal practice, part of the obligatory curriculum. Soil is a mixture of three components — sand, clay, and organics — the latter often called humus, not to be confused with hummus. Sand is very different from clay. It is not possible to bake bricks from sand. Sand needs a far higher temperature in an oven, and it inevitably would melt and end up as slag material. Contrary to popular belief, a cat's litter box is not filled with sand — sand does not absorb excretions. There is a special type of volcanic clay for that purpose, called attapulgite.

The flesh inside the mouth is sensitive and can distinguish different textures and materials well. It is easy to discern clay from sand in the mouth, because of the mineralogical difference between the two. Clay produces a slick sensation, while sand, on the other hand, scours the gums — the latter is even proverbial in Dutch.

With practice, it is possible to become a professional soil taster, discerning percentages of clay in a sample of up to 10 percent level of precision. I have known many soil-tasting researchers, and none experienced any side effects. Nowadays, professional tasting is replaced with objective laboratory analysis. Courses on the subject by oral intake are obsolete. Soil tasting had a long history, previously being taught in academies. The clay content of agricultural topsoil was, for many centuries before the introduction of fertilizer, a measure of field quality. Clay can absorb, and subsequently relinquish, not only water, but also essential nutrients for crop growth. Soil tasting, therefore, was a standard procedure in the assessment of land value for taxation, sale, or inheritance. This is still reflected in the Dutch word slikken, as a verb meaning "to take in", and as a plural noun meaning "mudflats." The singular noun slik means "mud," but in many Dutch dialects also "sweets for sucking."

Soil-tasting looks a lot like wine tasting; do not swallow after rolling the sample around in the mouth, but, rather, spit it out. There is however one drawback in soil tasting; the humic organic component is not easily detected, apparently because it is experienced by the mucosa, similarly to vegetable foods, and not being a mineral, it may contain germs and the eggs of organisms. It was these eggs that up to a half century ago posed a severe health risk to half of the country.

The Netherlands can be roughly split up into a clay-half (the northwestern part) and a sand-half (the southeastern part). It turned out that about half of the inhabitants on the sand-half suffered from permanent infection caused by intestinal worms, Ascaris roundworms. This parasitic worm can migrate through the human body causing all kinds of complications, some of them fatal. In those days, there were, of course, efficient cures to get rid of these unwelcome fellow travellers. I do remember one medicine in particular because it was chocolate flavoured, a rare treat during the war. A common practice at the time was to fertilize kitchen gardens with human manure, replete with Ascaris eggs. An unwashed garden harvest subsequently re-infected people with the Ascaris worm Ad infinitum. This did not affect people from the clay-half of Holland and, as a consequence, people living on clay ground were proverbially prosperous Dutchmen.

The cause of this difference must be found in the hygroscopic properties of clay minerals. Worm eggs from human manure will be rapidly desiccated in clay environments. Therefore it turned out that people living on clay grounds, once cured from a worm infection, were not re-infected.

I believe the benefits of soil in food are caused by the hygroscopic function of clay minerals. From times immemorial it has been daily practice for humans to eat unclean roots and vegetables, as well as meat seasoned with ash and accidental contaminants. Conventional cleaning habits are a recent introduction. I am not convinced that so-called "paleo-diets" are a real boost to human welfare; but clay soil may be a very real, if only minor, constituent of healthy, human food.

In this context, I would like to draw attention to a peculiar additive that has been on the market for more than a century, Luvos. Heilerde (healing earth) has been continuously on the market since 1918. So, what is Luvos? In fact, it is a type of soil called löss in German and Dutch. Widespread in middle latitudes, from Northern France and Belgium, eastward to middle Germany, Poland, Ukraine, Russia, and central China; it also covers extensive parts of the American Midwest and Argentina. In fact, this sediment is the most common superficial soil stratum on the land surface of the Earth. It is ubiquitous because deserts have been characteristic of the Quaternary geological period as much as ice caps. Desert dust has been, and still is transported worldwide by storms, especially during the ice ages, but also currently- red Saharan-dust regularly colours car roofs in Amsterdam, and it fertilizes the green roofs of buildings. Dust deracination is only absent in the Arctic and Antarctic regions. But it fertilizes all seas and oceans and is an important factor in the ecology of marine life. Löss dusts, like Luvos, consist of two distinct components: partly clay mineral, partly tiny splintery quartz sand grains — it is not pure clay. The sandy fraction makes it less slick than pure clay and easier to swallow.

Eating Luvos to prevent, or counteract, intestinal problems follows a much older tradition of soil consumption in the part of Holland where the topsoil consists of löss. This holds particularly true for the consumption of soil at St. Gerlach's in Limburg.

St. Gerlach was a repentant hermit, a holy man, living in a hollow oak tree around 1200. He became a local saint and was officially recognized by Pope Benedict XIII in 1728. The Saint's grave was excavated at the side of the Geul River, in löss soil, and people started to collect soil from this spot for consumption with the belief that it would give them good health. Over the course of time, a monastery for noblemen was built near the site, and in 1750 a church was erected (***) in Rococo style, which housed an impressive tomb for the Saint. Underneath this tomb, a space filled with soil was created. This St. Gerlach soil can be collected in little samples for personal or veterinary use (***). Nowadays, this is not the löss soil in which Saint Gerlach was interred. Present day pilgrims are provided with hygienic fine-grained white limestone sand from the cliffs bordering the Geul river valley to the south. The substitute completely lacks the absorbing properties of the preceding löss. Fine-grain limestone, i.e., chalk, is a well-known additive of rhubarb recipes to prevent kidney-stone formation. Prudent modern churchwardens knew the new chalk as an innocent mineral substance, harmless when consumed. The continued provision of St.

Gerlach soil in the church is now a manifestation of faith in sanctitude, and belief in the tonic values of tradition. These values also interact with practical medical effects of edible soil in the Netherlands.

OF ASYMMETRICAL LEGS, SCARS, INFRASTRUCTURES, AND EXILE.

FLORA REZNIK

If belonging is no longer a natural and immutable state (as most of us can probably attest, since most of us here speak a non-native language and live on foreign ground), what allows us to create strategies of belonging, these coalitions that hold human frailty?

Aren't we in need of a new definition of the friend-enemy distinction in order to survive?

In what way can precariousness mobilize us rather than petrify us?

What about escapism, resentment, and self-isolation as political emotions in times of extreme precarity?

What would be the purpose of a « fictive territory »?

Where or how does the grass roots, earthly aspect of partisan warfare resonate in market warfare?

What is the difference between making sense and interpreting?

Is my body my own landscape or part of other's?

Which trauma could the earth hide underneath its surface?

Having been atomized, and torn asunder politically by neoliberalism but also existentially by this 'reaction to alterity' (which might, in the end, be the root of so many evil-isms?), can we only hope to form a tough tissue that pulls us together, that signifies some kind of healing, however uncomfortable and imperfect?

While evoking apparently abstract notions of the mark and the re-mark here, we are also thinking about scars.
—Jacques Derrida, The Monolingualism of the Other, or The Prosthesis of Origin.

* *PROSTHETIC SELF.*

My brother's leg grows at a rhythm of its own, slower than the rest of his body. Through multiple surgeries, starting from when he was a baby up until his 18*th* year of age, my brother's femur reached a length almost equal to his other, leaving a scar and a small limp in his walk (amongst other things). The femur was cut in half and a needle was attached to either side of the bone. The two needles slid over each other, and thanks to a rudimentary mechanism of bolts and screws first, and a more sophisticated magnetic system later, the parts of the bone gradually separated. A gap of around two millimetres was created each day, and the bone tissue regenerated itself. The procedure had to go quickly, so the bone would remain soft, allowing for further stretching. Eventually, when the desired distance was achieved, the stretching ceased, while the needles continued to function as support until the bone solidified. As my brother kept growing, the difference between the two legs came back, so the procedure had to resume every couple of years.

The first rule of ethics, says Levinas, can be condensed into this simple phrase: 'After you, sir'. A scene comes to my mind: a person opening the door for another, and letting them pass through first. Where are they entering? Is it a house? Whose house? Obviously, the house of the person who is opening the door, otherwise the gesture would make no sense. The word 'home' adds to "house" a certain sense of ownership: it is a place that one inhabits and somehow feels like its own, and where one can have friends over as guests. *Every Man has a property in his own Person*[1], suggesting freedom comes to be linked with power and property: the power to do what one wills, in relation to one's body and actions without obstruction, as well as other properties like houses and objects. But Levinas proposes: *Morality begins when freedom, instead of being justified by itself, feels itself to be arbitrary and violent.*

1 This definition of freedom is present in John Locke's thought, and has influenced liberal political discourse ever since.

When alterity inhabits the body in such a way, a violence, a rupture of the cocoon that the self builds around itself *will have occurred*. This strange choice of tense points at a priority that is not chronological, but ontological. Alterity conditions identity fundamentally. This resistance to alterity that we might experience is a reaction to a condition of the self already always being open not *to* but *by* otherness.

Another option for my brother would have been to use a prosthetic. But the leg wasn't missing, so it would have been necessary to amputate. It was my parents' decision and I suppose there were more options. In a sense, the extension of the bone tissue is also a form of prosthetic leg, complicating the distinction between natural and artificial. The scar that my brother's leg bears is the material documentation of the inscription of alterity. A scar reminds us of the effort of a body to close its seams. The body something resists, and the continuity of the tissue is forever disrupted. The possibility of being open precedes that of being closed, and this is what operates the scarring. A scar is an unassimilable, hardly recognizable part of oneself that behaves in unpredictable ways and haunts the "healed" person with the memory of the open wound.

A prosthetic usually performs a double bind: it replaces a missing part of a body, defining that body with a lack, while it also denotes the unboundedness of the self. This second sense operates the entanglement of the body with an environment. A dear friend once exclaimed, without being able to hide the excitement caused by the realization when studying Merleau-Ponty: 'my body doesn't end at the tips of my fingers!' If this is so, then the world is no longer 'at hand,' available for manipulation. There is a point to be made about the prosthetic nature of selfhood in general, or logic of the supplement. The supplement doesn't replace anything original; it extends its inherent capacity to become other.

**CHANGE IN Y, CHANGE IN X.*

My brother's scar has been always more or less concealed from the public eye, under baggy pants and long swim shorts. My relationship with him was not of the public sort, we are bound in the private, intimate realm of the home. I saw the scar stretch as he grew, and new layers appear after each surgery. In my head, it resembled the bed of a river, ever changing under the surface.

Through a gesture of inversion, I transformed my brother's scar/river bed into a mountain chain. I played with scales to create a fictive territory and enabled my imagination to inhabit that place. An invitation to allow what marks us (his scar, that marked us both in different and indelible ways) to be bigger than ourselves. His body is a territory that conditions us in unintelligible ways. What would be the trace of this experience of exploring an artificial territory made to resemble (and differ from) the real scar of my brother, as an origin impossible to grasp? And the real scar, always mutating, stretching, twitching, folding, and unfolding, what does it have to do with this silicone mold, forever still, animated through photogrammetry? What does this copy translate, or better, what displacements does it facilitate? What is left to be said, when *something seems to* force me to keep on talking *about it / to it*? Could both be a political discourse, an infrastructural tool of imagination or a poem? A voice-over that emits no sound and only appears from time to time in subtitles, on a separate screen that might go unnoticed unless a small drifting of attention occurs:

Sister: can we talk about this?
Brother: can we?

-there is something inside me that grows at a rhythm of its own.
-we use so many other things to move.
-anyways it needed to be fixed.

-and what's outside?
-anestesia.

All again, all eternal, all entangled, interlocked, in love, oh, then...

-No, It's over.

And one day we created an island
out of conviction or faith
in an artificial world.

There's cut 1, cut 2.
Screw 1, screw 2.
-What creatures inhabit those slopes?

-For sure there is no more than 3 people there, and 3 sheep
longing for comfort,
normality.
No Tibetian monk in this island
living without pain in the here and now.

-here and now
-where is that?
-not here. Let's go.

(...)
Trace over trace. And even this can be erased.
-and then what?
-to go on, to climb up.
-a foot, another foot. What else?

Brother: That question does not exist in me, because my whole being is the answer.

-We just thought it would be better on the other side,
that the waters should open up.

* *THE TILLING OF THE GROUND.*

So much searching for a reconnection with nature these days. We feel out of touch. We've lost something. Once we are grounded, we will be safe. The pleasing view of tilled land organically produced nourishment. Planet Earth is the mother of Law, bestowing fair prizes to men that work its soil, distributing to each what they deserve! The roots of law and justice meet in the earth, and this juncture ensures that Law is just! *The taking of the soil is the primitive act that establishes the law. (...) [A] common primitive act, [based in which] a sort of supreme property of the community in its totality [is created]*[2]. This act of *original appropriation* haunts us in our dreams, it's an invisible wound we carry inside. We don't want the Law, we rebel, we want to believe that nobody took anything, or that we did it all together, and thus no laws would be necessary, we want to be free! We don't want to take responsibility for that appropriation, we don't want to feel the violence of freedom. And then we are grounded, like children grounded by their parents, in a state of redemptive innocence.

This "internal measure" of Justice shows itself in the fixed lines (the marks in the ploughed soil) that express the divisions that assure the orderly functioning of human coexistence. This is the only legitimate origin of Law, from which any later law derives. There is a determined relationship between such an orderly soil and the disorderly sea, of the exteriority, a sphere where the free contact between people occurs. *The ships that cross the seas do not leave traces;* they are not like the furrows in the ploughed soil that allow the juridical order. That is why it is not possible to establish laws that regulate the relationships between different peoples. Man is a wolf to man in the natural state before Law tames him. Thus, the foreigner becomes an enemy, someone that can be dealt with only through force.

The enemy is simply the other, the foreigner, and it is enough that he is existentially, in a particularly intensive sense, something other or foreign, so that in an extreme case it would be possible that a conflict with him would not be decided through a normative system [...] The alterity of the foreigner in the concrete existing conflict means the negation of one's own mode of existence.

The ploughed soil is a mythical past that stands for another metaphor: the "lines of friendship." They delimit a society of friends (inside), and of enemies (outside). *The capacity to recognize a iustus hostis is the principle of all law of nations.* Inside, it is always possible to recognize the traces of the past and retreat towards the origin of the community. Outside, it is the Other, the unpredictable, the contamination of the ships that cross the ocean leaving no permanent trace. These lines need to be enacted *constantly,* drawing from the historical experience of war where this mythical distinction expresses itself, by a Sovereign decision. The experience of war needs to be constantly reminded, always a real possibility on the horizon. To lose this would be catastrophic because nothing else could justify the sovereign decision and the Law he enacts. The inside must remain clearly separated from the outside. War defends an original "way of life," proper to the community, and that distinguishes it from its enemies. This is fundamental to the power of the (liberal) State that the sovereign decision must manifest or re-enact.

Can "humanity" then be a political concept? This would ruin the essential friend-enemy distinction. This situation coincides with "the war of partisans," a

2 I'll be following Carl Schmitt's thoughts in these paragraphs. What appears in italics are citations directly from his texts. He was an influential German jurist and political thinker (and, important to note, a prominent member of the Nazi party) who wrote during a large part of the 20th Century. He founded the first corollary of *The Nomos of the Earth in the International Law of Jus Publicum Europaeum*. His thoughts remain relevant for numerous philosophers and political theorists, including Giorgio Agamben, Hannah Arendt, Walter Benjamin, Susan Buck-Morss, Jacques Derrida, Jürgen Habermas, Chantal Mouffe, Antonio Negri, and Slavoj Žižek, among others.

manifestation of "absolute hostility" towards the Political. In partisan warfare, the concepts tend to dissolve; the traditional criteria to identify an enemy are destabilized: the partisans do not wear a uniform, they intend to go unnoticed, they are not an identifiable soldier that could be killed in a battle. Their mode of fighting is disseminated; it extends indefinitely in time and space. The partisans are not necessarily nationalists, but civilians help them, because they have an earthly connection to their land. Through this type of war, there is a setback to telluric determination of the commons, of the social: an iteration of the Aristotelian paradigm of the *ethos*. *Ethos* is what ties *physis* (nature / place) with *nomos* (law). This brings the Political to unclear limits, and it could even render it superfluous.

This would be ruinous to the political because *ethos* is ontologically prior to sovereignty, and therefore puts sovereignty's unconditionality into question. Through this telluric set back, the decision about what defines the commons, a national identity *(the ethos of a people)* is left in the hands of myth alone.

The alternatives seem to be either it is the sovereign, or the *ethos* who must secure the *juncture* of the *physis* and the *nomos* and thus define the lines of friendship, essential to the functioning of a society.

*TRACES.

Back to the image of the tilled land, rows of lines that are products of hard labor under the sun and the snow, drawn over and over on the soil across the ages. But the workers of the land have seldom owned the land. They seldom fully enjoyed the products of the land, and this has always been protected by the same laws that are supposed to emanate from this very action of tilling. These traces are re-enacted by labour only as long as the law obliges the peasant to comply. Could this be the origin of the legitimacy of the sovereign's decision?

The trace[3] does not show an origin, but it replaces it: such is the logic of the supplement and of the prosthetics. A trace is always a trace of a trace. A trace is the mark of a subtraction, which ruins all attempts to regain an origin: nobody can re-present a mythical origin, because it was never present. The trace does not allow for a thinking of community in terms of a shared *ethos*, nor does it allow a sovereign decision to determine the inside from the outside based on some supposedly natural lines that delimit what is proper to the people either.

A territory (and a body/territory) is always and crucially appropriated land, its limits are defined by trespassing. The decision of the sovereign is still necessary, but it lacks the unconditionality that gave him the prerogative of performing the jointure of *physis* and *nomos*. From now on, *physis* is the muddy ground of sedimented historical social meanings as well as the uncontrollable powers of nature: the dirt on which we stand, which conditions us and with which we need to negotiate.

What is the "real possibility" that obsesses (hante) Schmitt, or that inhabits him, but the very law of spectrality? The oscillation and the association, the conjunctive-disjunction that ties together the real effectivity and the possibility. Behold how it assembles and dislocates at once.

A thought about this *juncture* that separates while holding together would be a philosophy trespassing its limits, of undoing its seams and opening the wound: a thought forced to become political, but political in a different

3 We will be following the thought of Jacques Derrida on the notion of "trace" and on his critique of Carl Schmitt's political theory. The sentences marked in italics are citations from his texts.

sense. The notion of critique is key here. The very instance of the *krinein* or the crisis in which the decision of the sovereign is called for implies now the impossibility of a clear distinction: the establishment of the line that separates something from something else follows the ruinous logic of the trace, which erases itself, which does not allow for the identification of the original that it supposedly refers. It is a decision over something undecidable.

A thought concerned with working on the conditions that constrain it with the intention of trespassing those limits, of thinking something *else,* would be the only form of critical thought and decision making, at the price of losing the criteria for that critique. It would be an affected thought, a thought forced to venture towards uncertain territories. This step towards the *other* of thought, its blind spot, is towards what the Western tradition has left outside its area of concern. "The Political," then, from this new perspective, would be a certain thing which is difficult to name, that haunts philosophy and deprives it from its fundamentals.

The political remains linked to sovereignty (an instance of arbitrary and contingent decision) as opposed to the mythical *ethical fundament* and its ally, the notion of *humanity*. Politics must be based on historical grounds that can be worked on, not on transcendental, untouchable mythical notions. But sovereignty cannot be unconditioned. As much as it is a political thought, it also deals with material conditions. If it aims to be critical, it works towards modifying those conditions, but without any assurance that their criteria are correct. "The other" can be a figure of these conditions, as this notion extends beyond and exceeds the human, or beyond what can be recognized as human. But how can one be responsible for what cannot be known or recognized, not even as a "fellow Human?"

* VULNERABILITY AND INFRASTRUCTURE.

Partisan warfare resonates remarkably with current times in which new forms of market warfare coexist with more traditional forms of war. In the market warfare, crises have become tools of governance, rendering it impossible to recognize one crisis as the ultimate crisis, the decisive one. Instead, cyclic, or induced crises, follow one another in an endless loop taking populations as hostages. Bodies assemble based not on knowledge or recognition, but on shared vulnerability in the context of current neo-liberalism and its politics of precarity[4]. This vulnerability is what is common, and constitutes bodies as relational entities, while a specific political system unequally distributes precarity. An actual infrastructure of support is precisely what is at stake, as opposed to mythical and unchangeable lines of friendship.

A valuable assembly is one that looks for ways to contribute to the making of infrastructure that would enable ways of passing, of moving through a space without obstruction, harassment, administrative detention, or fear of injury or death. *The pavement and the street are already to be understood as requirements of the body as it exercises its rights of mobility. They themselves become part of the action and not only its support (...) The political meaning of the human body [is that] part of what a body is, is its dependency on other bodies and networks of support.*

Indeed, if the vulnerable body here stands as an ontological category, it is, in the sense of a social ontology, a political body, which is defined by the

4 We will now follow Judith Butler's thoughts on vulnerability, precarity and the notion of infrastructure as the material social networks of support, as opposed to mythical lines of friendship. The sentences marked in italics are citations from her texts.

relations that make its own life and actions passable/possible and sustainable in a certain context. These relationships are historically and economically specific. This extends to relations with other humans, as much as living processes and inorganic conditions that are vehicles for living. These are nonhuman dimensions of human survival.

It is not as "humans" that we are bound together, but human animals whose survival depends on the workable political organization of social conditions of both unwilled proximity and interdependency.

Now, this vulnerability is not always recognized, and this is what determines the level of precarity of a subject of population. And it is irreducible to recognition, which posits a crucial challenge to democracy insofar it is understood as a *politics of representation*. Politics must then be related to *the other of the communitarian*, what forces it open. A situation in which the vulnerability of a body fails to be recognized (and thus becomes disposable, as an extension of war machinery, for example) is not solely the result of an individual act of blindness or bad faith, but also, and most importantly, it involves power dynamics that differentially produce bodies (individuals or entire populations) as more precarious than others.

It should be noted that there is a difference between *recognition* and *apprehension:* the latter would be a form of noticing what is irreducible to knowledge, or, better put, what exists at the margins of socially recognized knowledge, produced as a spectre of what lies inside the frame. *Recognizability is by no means a given,* it is not because an-other *appears* in front of me, that *I* have the means to recognize her as an equal, from the perspective of the self. The conditions for this *appearance* need to be produced.

Interdependency is not always some harmonious state of coexistence. There is no way to dissociate dependency from aggression. Apprehension is not the name of a gentle, caring gesture for the brother in need: instead, it is an obligation, a responsibility towards another who we do not know and who puts the "we" into question. Interdependency might be a name for coalitions that are made out of necessity and with great deals of compromise, and that *solidarity emerges from this rather than from deliberate agreements we enter knowingly.* The collective assembling of bodies that matter *press[es] up against the limits of social recognizability.* This is indeed a precarious state of being, but one that can mobilize forces and act upon the infrastructure that needs to be reworked, the infrastructure that defines the "we" in very concrete terms: that enables some to pass and be part of a network of care and support, and some to remain outside.

Belonging is no longer a natural and immutable state, and therefore needs to be reframed as strategies of belonging. We are diasporic creatures, exiled since birth, because the land on which we stand is not ours, nor has it belonged to our ancestors. What constitutes us is "*After you*", a gesture towards another. We are here as second inhabitants. We can't rely on an attachment to this or that land: the land *will have been* since always reworked, tilled by other hands, nourished by rain and worms and cycles that are beyond our powers of appropriation. Strategies of belonging relate to labour, to the artificiality of a shared effort to affiliate less to a time and place, than to a cause that aims at transcending that time and place *because* it acts upon them, transforming them.

* EXILE.

For some reason, *The Monolingualism of the Other* is the first text I read by Derrida. He writes in French and speaks about the French language, which I don't understand. I read it in Spanish:

Me pregunto si se puede amar, gozar, orar, reventar de dolor o reventar a secas en otra lengua o sin decir nada de ello a nadie, sin siquiera hablar. / I wonder if one can love, feel pleasure, pray, burst in pain or simply burst in another language or even without saying anything about it to anyone else, without even speaking.

In this book, he performs an autobiography of sorts. Growing up in Algeria, in a Jewish family, he spoke French at home and in school, but was denied the possibility of speaking Arabic (which is what all his friends spoke on the street or the football courts). His mother tongue didn't help him when he was expelled from the Licée due to an anti-Semitic quota implemented by the Vichy regime. It was only later in life that he became a Franco-Maghrebian, regaining French citizenship, showing that citizenship "does not always define a cultural, linguistic or historical participation." He writes that he has only one language, where he is at home and that constitutes who he is: the French language. Yet despite this, he goes on to say – in French – that French isn't his language, it is not his to own. Stepping ahead of his opponents, he admits to performing a practical contradiction. He is used to the threats: "If you continue like this, you will be put in the Rhetorics Faculty, or even Literature. The punishment or exile could be even worse if you insist," he paraphrases. The threat promises exile as the horrifying possibility of silence, of not being able to speak in one's own tongue. But, as Derrida has warned, he has never owned a language to begin with. His discourse constantly operates through translation.

Many years later, while reading *The Beast and the Sovereign,* also by Derrida, I noticed that this text contained sentences that didn't always make complete sense on their own, something was purposely postponed; *it* came constantly as waves that didn't resolve completely but that dissolve in the one that follows, accumulating into a somewhat diffuse sedimentation of meaning. Those waves seemed to carry with them debris, tiny bits of information that had fallen off structures of belonging (the sentences where they were first included). "We are shortly going to show this," he would say, meaning: "I will come back to this later," and then *it* would, and whatever could be grasped would come without announcing that it would come back. Like the "pas du loup," the "step of the wolf" or the "non-wolf" (the book is busy with the figure of the wolf ubiquitous in the Western tradition of Political Philosophy): a wolf so quiet that you don't see it trespass. I found that to be a beautiful lesson. Perhaps the experience of reading, and of course of thinking, was not meant to be like the instantaneous consumption of a product, but rather a more complicated experience of trying to *make* sense. To produce sense, rather than to interpret, and this would always be a collective and thus a political task regarding infrastructures of care and strategies of belonging.

ACKNOWLEDGEMENTS

by Flora Reznik

About four years ago an invitation from a stranger sent me on a trip that would open opportunities for my questions and practice exponentially. A trip that transformed my practice inside out. Someone, to whom I will be forever thankful, seemed to trust me after only seeing a work of mine and sharing a couple of coffees in the context of an exhausting art exhibition. These are the sorts of encounters that have marked my life, and opened unexpected doors for me to experiment in new and challenging ways. And most importantly, have reaffirmed a belief that trust from/to a stranger can be a powerful tool for change and betterment, both at an individual and societal level.

Some months later I would find myself driving and living in a 10 meter long bus (an old mobile supermarket), through Friesland, a land I had never set foot in before, alone, with a language I did not understand, but with the support of an extremely generous art initiative that encouraged me to be playful and "think big". In 2019 I was gifted the opportunity to develop Unknown Grounds, a performative symposium that would address the notion of "Iepen Mienskip" (Open Community) proposed by the 2018 Leeuwarden European Capital of Culture, this time through a joint effort of Tresoar Leeuwarden and VHDG. The aim was to generate a platform for collective thought based in Leeuwarden that would examine the link between territoriality and community and how we can create shared meanings. We dared to question the ground on which we stood. Instead of being a solid fundament that we take for granted, we proposed conceiving "ground" as something unknown, and open to inquiry from multiple disciplines and personal experiences.

I was surprised and extremely happy to find out that the open call for participants to take part in the Unknown Grounds performative-symposium in 2019 attracted enthusiastic and varied reactions. It transpired that we managed to gather not just people interested in a certain topic, but practitioners from different disciplines who all, or almost all, worked with "ground" in one way or another. This meant that a true community was born, and the breaks in between the planned activities were filled with effervescent conversations. Everyone was curious about what the other was doing because each new perspective enriched and broadened their own. The energy was vibrant and the program was brought to life by truly engaged participants. Far from the 'speaker on the platform / listeners on their seats taking notes' traditional symposium, the event felt more like a collective knowledge-sharing performance, a playful co-educational platform. I applaud the adventurous spirit of the participants and the guests, and I can't wait to meet some of you again soon, and to welcome new curious minds to the game.

Almost two years have passed since Unknown Grounds I, and we are now busy with preparations for the second edition. This publication made itself wait. It's probably a cliche to even mention this, but in a time when everything moves fast (often too fast) books are a refuge for some of us. And I like to think that they are also a political gesture: they offer resistance to an economy of fast food, fast fashion and populist slogans. Books stand there, cumbersome, like a big pink elephant in a room, claiming that we take the time to read them. And even if they lay in the bookshelf of a private home, books are places of encounter. A fundamental element of resistance to the powerful attempts to atomize us. We never read alone. Reading is a public event. Much like in Bolaño's novels, books are responsible for forming some of the strongest friendships around a mutual fascination, or even love, for a certain writer or poet, alongside a political struggle that is enacted not only with ideas, but also with passion. We read, we write and we discuss with passion. There's no more important fuel for these activities.

At this point, I want to thank some people by their names. Lieselot Van Damme for letting me into VHDG's world and offering such great guidance, Bert Looper for sharing his precious time and trusting a young foreigner with such a big responsibility, Agnes Winter, moderator of the event and current director of VHDG who accompanied me throughout the process of the making of this publication and with who I will continue to work with for the coming editions of Unknown Grounds, Nia Konstantinova for being the best producer I could ever have dreamt of and for bringing Nathaniel Feldmann into the game, who gave shape to the Script for a Synthetic Play and a big part of its fictional/playful spirit.

My thanks go also to our dear guests, the authors of such insightful and beautiful texts and visual essays, who each committed to this project beyond expectations: Bert Looper (again), masharu, Sissel Marie Tonn, Ribal El-Khatib, Theun Karelse, and Andrej Radman. Bert Boekschoten, our bonus contributor (he was not present during the event but one of his texts forms part of this publication).

Thanks to Yun Lee who created and operated the soundscape for our two days journey into the unknown, and to Ansito and Johan de Vries who worked on the lighting. A big shout out to Tresoar's workers and volunteers without whom we would have most definitely not managed to pull this off: Bob Kuipers, Barbara van Rijn, Sieger Visser, Aukje Bosch, Tjesje Gerlsma. Thanks to Marie Sledsens, who jumped on this train and made a first draft design for this publication, and later Wibke Bramesfeld, who gave final form to the beautiful object which you now hold in your hands.

Thank you Freek Lomme, director of Onomatopee for believing in this project and caring for it until its birth as a book, and Amy Gowen, for lovingly providing us with her editorial advice.

And of course, the participants of the performative simposium Unknown Grounds, whose engagement gave life to this project: Suzanne Bernhardt, Doke Pauwels, Koen Bartijn, Victoria Douka-Doukopoulou, Berbee, Katja Verheul, Sylvie Arrabito, Evelijn Martinius, Levin Stein, Eef Veldkamp, Valentina Vella, Witold van Ratingen, Alex Vanderbeld, Lola Diaz Contoni, Frederiek Benema, Ellen Mandemaker, Roza Kootstra, S.J. Snow, Margriet van Weenen, Ingeborg Entrop and Anna-Rosja Haveman.

APPENDIX

APPENDIX I

Context note

by Lieselot van Damme, former director of art initiative VHDG and Bert Looper, former director of Tresoar Frysk Histoarysk en Letterkundich Sintrum

Dear reader,

Thank you for joining us in the unknown. I would like to take some time to provide context on how Unknown Grounds came into being. Although the event is brand new, it is the result of a two-year collaboration between Stichting VHDG and a selected artist.

In 2017, VHDG invited Flora Reznik to be the third driver in the annual Artist in Residence (AIR) project: VHDG/SRV, where invited an artist to live, work, and travel in our SRV-van for six weeks. With a maximum speed of 25 km/p/h they were asked to explore Friesland, the 12-meter-long vehicle acting as a mobile studio. The residency concluded with an exhibition that presented the newly made work.

VGDH met Flora at Art Rotterdam 2017, where she presented her installation *Hole*, a hole she had dug every weekend, for eight months, at the 'Zandmotor' in Den Hague. She presented the work as a combination of art, poetry, science, and philosophy in an eloquent and accessible, yet deeply evocative manner. I knew the moment I saw the project that she was the perfect candidate for the next SRV residency.

In the autumn of 2017, Flora travelled through Friesland in the SRV-van, exploring the notions of ground and territory; asking questions, such as: *How is identity formed by the ground we walk and live on?* She remodelled the van to an agricultural digging machine and approached farmers, gardeners and landowners asking: *Can I swap some of your land with the land of someone you do not know?* After the swap of a square of soil she dug, both parties signed a 'ruilverkaveling' contract. This contract was based on a historical document that Flora found in the Tresoar archives[1]; a legal contract that had been used centuries ago to (re)divide property in Friesland.

Flora's journey concluded with the exhibition *Immovable property*, at VHDG's exhibition space. Both VHDG and Bert Looper, director of Tresoar, felt strongly that this topic had much more depth to be explored, and decided to become partners in a new collaboration.

In 2018, Leeuwarden/Friesland became the European Cultural Capital, grounded on the main theme – *Iepen Mienskip* (Open Community). The theme sparked many discussions among inhabitants and in the cultural field that continue to echo today. What does 'Iepen Mienskip' mean? Is it actually a bold statement, implying that the Mienskip was once closed? If so, then what does it mean to open a community? We felt that an in-depth debate was missing.

In the context of Friesland, one's identity is not only shaped by the local community, but even more so by the type of ground one grows and lives on. The perspective from Flora's research, in collaboration with Tresoar, offers new insights regarding Iepen Mienskip. This became the baseline for Unknown Grounds.

We look forward to embarking on this journey into unknown territories together.

1 Tresoar is the repository of the history of Fryslân. Its archive contains countless newspapers and magazines published in Fryslân, hundreds of thousands of books including some books from the library of Erasmus, photos, films, sound recordings, court reports, legal deeds, Blaeu's Atlas, manuscripts and letters by famous Frisians, the company archives of Douwe Egberts and archives of the Eleven (Frisian) Cities Association , CDs ranging from Frisian punk to Classical, a manuscript of "Noctes Atticae" made by monks and dating back to 836 AD and well over 150 bibliographies composed by J.J. Kalma and the oldest and most recent Frisian literature and scientific publications, both in physical and digital support.

APPENDIX II

References from the Contributor's Texts

REFERENCES FROM DAILY RESEARCH BY SISSEL MARIE TONN

Doing easy – William S. Burroughs. (2016, July 1). Library of Babel. https://tayiabr.wordpress.com/2016/07/01/doing-easy-william-s-burroughs/

REFERENCES FROM GROUNDLESS GROUNDS BY ANDREJ RADMAN

The first version of this essay appears under the title of "3D Perception ≠ 2D Image + 1D Inference: Or Why a Single Precise Shot Would Often Miss the Target, whereas a Series of Imprecise Shots Will Eventually Lead to a Hit" in What Images Do, eds. J. Bäcklund, H. Oxvig, M. Renner and M. Søberg (Aarhus: Aarhus University Press, 2019), 145–55

1. James J. Gibson, The Ecological Approach to Visual Perception (New Jersey: Lawrence Erlbaum Associates, 1986), 242.
2. Michel Serres, "Birth," in The Five Senses: A Philosophy of Mingled Bodies (New York: Continuum, 2008), 17–23.
3. Gregory Bateson, Steps to an Ecology Of Mind: Collected Essays in Anthropology, Psychiatry, Evolution, and Epistemology (New York: Ballantine, 1972), 318. Cf. Maurice Merleau-Ponty, Phenomenology of Perception (London: Routledge & Keagan Paul, 1962), 152.
4. Maxine Sheets-Johnstone, The Primacy of Movement (Aarhus: Aarhus University Department of Philosophy, 1999), 139, 146–50. See also: Maxine Sheets-Johnstone, ed. The Corporeal Turn: An Interdisciplinary Reader (Exeter: Imprint Academic, 2009).
5. Gilles Deleuze, Cinema 1: The MovementDImage (London: The Athlone Press, 1986), 56.
6. Pierre Lévy's expression from Félix Guattari, Chaosmosis: An Ethico-Aesthetic Paradigm (Bloomington: Indiana University Press, 1995), 108.
7. Gibson was well aware of the philosophical implications of his work. As the Gibsonian Edward Reed explains, by the time Gibson obtained his B.A. in philosophy in 1925, such great thinkers as John Dewey, William James, Bertrand Russell and Alfred North Whitehead had all struggled with this problem of body/mind dualism: "Once a dualism was erected it seemed impossible to eliminate it: If matter is purely physical, then how can aggregates of matter evolve into minds (and surely the brain–mere matter–is the basis of mind)? Yet, if awareness is purely mental, of what relevance to it are the physical trappings of the body?" See: Edward Reed, James J. Gibson and the Psychology of Perception (New Haven: Yale University Press, 1988), 287. James J. Gibson, Reasons for Realism: Selected Essays of James J. Gibson, ed. Edward S. Reed and Rebecca Jones (Hillsdale, NJ: L. Erlbaum, 1982), 415.
8. James J. Gibson, "On the Concept of Formless Invariants in Visual Perception," in Reasons for Realism: Selected essays of James J. Gibson, ed. Edward S. Reed and Rebecca Jones (Hillsdale, NJ: L. Erlbaum, 1982), 286.
9. Which, in turn, is recently challenged by 'the third kind' of image. See for example: Patricia Pisters, The NeuroDImage (Stanford: Stanford University Press, 2012).
10. Deleuze is referring to the first chapter of Henri Bergson, Matter and Memory (London: George Allen & Unwin, 1911).
11. "The act of picking up information . . . is a continuous act, an activity that is ceaseless and unbroken. The sea of energy in which we live flows and changes without sharp breaks. Even the tiny fraction of this energy that affects the receptors in the eyes, ears, nose, mouth, and skin is a flux, not a sequence. The exploring, orienting, and adjusting of these organs sink to a minimum during sleep but do not stop dead. Hence, perceiving is a stream, and William James's description of the stream of consciousness applies to it. Discrete perception, like discrete ideas, are as mythical as the Jack of Spades." Gibson, Ecological Approach, 240. Cf. William James, "The Stream of Thought," chap. 9 in The Principles of Psychology (London: Macmillan and Co., 1890), 224–90.
12. Peirce placed icons under Firstness, indices under Secondness and symbols under Thirdness.

13. Charles S. Peirce, "The Architecture of Theories," in Philosophical Writings of Peirce, ed. J. Buchler (New York: Dover Publications, 1955), 322.
14. Deleuze, Cinema 1, 56.
15. Behaviorist psychologists solved the problem of dualism by eliminating all concepts of mind and explaining them away as forms of behavior. Conversely, the Gestaltists made a fundamental mistake of treating observers as passive recipients of stimuli. Their approach was essentially naivistic, explaining perception by means of innate principles of organization. An insightful comparison of the two parallel traditions was provided by Paul Stenner in his lecture on "Deep Empiricism" at A Topological Approach to Cultural Dynamics Conference, Changing Cultures: Cultures of Change (Barcelona, December 9–12, 2009).
16. "Difference is not diversity. Diversity is given, but difference is that by which the given is given as diverse. Difference is not phenomenon but the noumenon closest to the phenomenon." Gilles Deleuze, Difference and Repetition (New York: Columbia University Press, 1994), 202.
17. Gibson, Ecological Approach, 233.
18. Realist in the sense that it is asymptotic to the contingent reality that drives the universe, and speculative in the sense of not driven by our reflection but by the exteriority and contingency of a universe that always antedates and postdates us.
19. Reza Negarestani, "Frontiers of Manipulation," Speculations on Anonymous Materials Symposium (2014), http://www.youtube.com/watch?v=Fg01MebGt9I (accessed July 6, 2019).
20. The thesis was set out by Gibson in his earlier book: James J. Gibson, The Senses Considered as Perceptual Systems (Boston: Houghton Mifflin, 1966).
21. Gilles Deleuze, The Fold: Leibniz and the Baroque (London: Athlone, 1993), 107. "Conscious perception is always a hallucination which refers back to differential relations established between minute perceptions, and that these perceptions express only affections of our material bodies by other material things, never in the form of complete objects, but as 'molecular movements.'"
22. Brian Massumi, "The Thinking-Feeling of What Happens: A Semblance of Conversation," Inflexions: A Journal for Research Creation 1, "How is Research-Creation?" (May 2008): 39.
23. Steven Shaviro, "The Actual Volcano: Whitehead, Harman, and the problem of Relations," in The Speculative Turn: Continental Materialism and Realism, ed. Levi Bryant, Nick Srnicek and Graham Harman (Melbourne: re.press, 2011), 291.
24. By "mentalism" Gibson means the approach which appeals to mental representations whereby each of us supposedly builds up his or her own cognitive map of the real world, based on his or her relation to it. It is allegedly this cognitive map or representation we are aware of, not the world itself. Gibson, Ecological Approach, 235.
25. Brian Massumi, A User's Guide to Capitalism and Schizophrenia: Deviations from Deleuze and Guattari
26. (Cambridge, MA: MIT, 1993), 99.
27. Gibson, Ecological Approach, 129.
28. Karl Popper, "The Bucket and the Searchlight: Two Theories of Knowledge," in The Philosophy of Ecology: From Science to Synthesis, ed. D.R. Keller and F.B. Golley (Athens, GA: The University of Georgia Press, 2000), 141–46.
29. Under the Western metaphysics of presence, or the privileging of the logos, everything that appears is determined or synthesized in advance from some prior ground. For Plato, this ground or source of appearing, or what allowed sensation to make sense, was the logos, that which could be said of anything, that which would remain the same (Heidegger's onto-theology).
30. Western ocularcentricity has blinded us and prevented from considering other senses. The tendency to privilege the sight as the sense that gives us access to the truth has been elaborated by Martin Jay, Downcast Eyes: The Denigration of Vision in Twentieth-Century French Thought (Berkeley: University of California Press, 1994).
31. Gregory Flaxman, "Introduction," in The Brain is the Screen: Deleuze and the Philosophy of Cinema, ed. G. Flaxman (Minneapolis: Minnesota University Press, 2000), 12–15. Cf.

Gilles Deleuze, Cinema 2: The Time-Image (London: Athlone Press, 1989), 27.
32. See contributions by Hal Foster, Martin Jay, Jonathan Crary, Rosalind Krauss, Norman Bryson and Jacqueline Rose in Hal Foster, ed., Vision and Visuality (Seattle: Bay Press, 1988).
33. In his Neuromancer (1984), William Gibson defined cyberspace as "consensual hallucination" where all the media converge. In this (cyber)space, computer "cowboys" travel disembodied across the world of data. See: Christine M. Boyer, CyberCities: Visual Perception in the Age of Electronic Communication (New York: Princeton Architectural Press, 1996), 14: "From the moment William Gibson announced in his dystopian science-fiction account Neuromancer (1984) that the new informational network or computer matrix called cyberspace looks like Los Angeles seen from five thousand feet up in the air, there has been a predilection for drawing a parallel between the virtual space of computer networks and post-urban places . . ." Cf. William Gibson, Neuromancer (New York: Ace Science Fiction, 1984).
34. Gibson, Ecological Approach, 63. It calls to mind a Žižekian story about a drunkard who lost his car keys in the dark but looked for them under the streetlight.

REFERENCES FROM UNKNOWN WORDS, UNKNOWN GROUNDS. LANGUAGE, LANDSCAPE, AND MEMORY BY BERT LOOPER

1. Lemaire, Ton, Ambo, 2002.
2. Postma, Obe, 1949.
3. Robert Macfarlance, Penguin Books Ltd, 2016.
4. Vries, Oebele, Uitgeverij Noordboek, 2012.
5. Rackham, Oliver, . London: J.M. Dent & Sons, 1986.

REFERENCES FROM MACHINE WILDERNESS BY THEUN KARELSE

Clark, Kenneth, Landscape into art, Ed. J. Murray, London, 1949.

REFERENCES FROM MUSEUM OF EDIBLE EARTH BY MASHARU

1. P.W. Abrahams. Soils: their implications to human health. The Science of the Total Environment. 291: 1-32, 2002.
2. Diagnostic and Statistical Manual of Mental Disorders (DSM-V). American Psychiatric Association. 2013.
Noortje M. Reeuwijk et al., Levels of lead, arsenic, mercury and cadmium in clays for oral use on the Dutch market and estimation of associated risks in Food Additives and Contaminants Part A. 29-66, 2013.
3. Henry, Jacques M. and F. Daniel Cring. Geophagy An Anthropological Perspective. 185, 2012.
4. Eric C. Brevik and Alfred E. Hartemink. History, Philosophy, and Sociology of Soil Science in Soils, Plant Growth and Crop Production, W. Verheye (Ed.). Encyclopedia of Life Support Systems (EOLSS), 21, 2010.
5. Parochie St. Gerlach te Houthem. http://www.st-gerlach.nl/pages/pelgrimage.htm. Accessed 03 April 2017.
6. Sera L. Young, Craving Earth: Understanding Pica - the Urge to Eat Clay, Starch, Ice, and Chalk. 46, 2011.
7. Sera L. Young, A Vile Habit? The potential biological consequences of geophagia, with special attention to iron in Consuming the Inedible: Neglected Dimensions of Food Choice, Jeremy M. MacClancy and Jeya Henry [Ed.] 2007.
8. Eating Clay: Lessons on Medicine from Worldwide Cultures. Enviromedica. http://www.enviromedica.com/eating-clay. Accessed 03 April 2017.

REFERENCES FROM OF ASYMMETRICAL LEGS, SCARS, INFRASTRUCTURE AND EXILE BY FLORA REZNIK

All the quotes from books by Derrida in this text were first extracted from Spanish versions of these books. The translations to English were made by me. As for useful reference, I list the titles of the works in English.

1. Emmanuel Lévinas, Totality and Infinity: An Essay on Exteriority, Pittsburgh, Pennsylvania: Duquesne University Press, 1969.
2. John Locke, The Second Treatise of Government. Indianapolis: Bobbs-Merrill, 1952.
3. Jacques Derrida, "Letter to a Japanese friend", in Derrida and Differance, ed. Wood & Bernasconi, Warwick, Parousia Press, 1985.
4. Jacques Derrida, "Autoimmunity: Real and Symbolic Suicides" in Giovanna Borradori, Philosophy in a Time of Terror, Ed. The University of Chicago Press, Chicago, 2003.
5. Jacques Derrida, "Force of law: the metaphysical foundation of authority", In Drucilla Cornell, Michel Rosenfeld & David Carlson (eds.), Deconstruction and the Possibility of Justice. Ed. Routledge, 1992.
6. Jacques Derrida, The politics of friendship, Ed. Verso, 2006.
7. Carl Schmitt, Political Theology, Four Chapters on the Concept of Sovereignty, Translated by George Schwab, MIT Press, Massachusetts, 1988.
8. Jacques Derrida, The politics of friendship.
9. Judith Butler, Frames of War, When is life grievable?, Verso, 2010.
10. Judith Butler, Notes toward a performative theory of assembly, Cambridge, Mass.: Harvard University Press, 2015.

APPENDIX III

Presentations of Contributors Translated to English and Bios

Hello, welcome everyone to Tresoar, Treasury of Friesland, which is the repository of the history of Friesland. I am Bert Looper, director of this institution, and historian by profession. I am very glad to be among all of you, and I am excited to discuss the notion of open community.

Bert Looper studied medieval history in Groningen and attended the Rijks Archiefschool in The Hague. Since 2007 to 2020 he has been the director of Tresoar, Frisian historical and literary centre. He has published on archivists, city history, Hanze, twentieth-century design and Frisian history. In 2017 he published *Here lies the sea (Hier ligt de zee)* a report of a lifelong search on the relationship between language, landscape, art, memory, and identity, spread across twenty essays. Against the background of the tension in Europe between modern state contexts and regions with its own history, Bert Looper takes the reader to an area that questions identity over many centuries.

My name is masharu, I am an earth lover. I would like to share with you an eating earth practice, and it's up to you, if you choose to take part or not.

masharu is a creative with a background in science. masharu's projects combine scientific research with a personal approach and cultural practices. In 2011 they obtained a PhD in Mathematics and graduated with honors from Photo Academy Amsterdam. In 2013–2014 they participated in the artist-in-residency programme at Rijksakademie van Beeldende Kunst in Amsterdam. In 2018 they were an artist fellow at the Netherlands Institute for Advanced Study in the Humanities and Social Sciences (NIAS-KNAW). Their artistic as well as scientific work has been exhibited, screened and published in various countries, including Austria, Belgium, China, Croatia, Cuba, Denmark, France, Germany, Guatemala, Indonesia, the Netherlands, Nigeria, Portugal, Russia, Spain, Suriname, Ukraine, UK and USA in such venues and events as African Artists' Foundation in Lagos, Spanish Cultural Centre in Guatemala City, World Design Event in Eindhoven, ReadyTex Gallery in Paramaribo, 4th Jakarta Contemporary Ceramics Biennale in Jakarta, European Ceramic Workcentre in Oisterwijk, Sustainica in Dusseldorf, the 6th Moscow Biennale of Contemporary Arts in Moscow and Museo Maritimo in Bilbao.

Hello everyone, my name is Ribal, an Architect and an asylum seeker in the Netherlands, so I'm living here temporarily and hoping that I can stay. I'm from the unknown! Literally from the Unknown!! I will leave the rest for my speech tomorrow and will talk more about it then, see you tomorrow.

Ribal El-Khatib is an Assistant Architect, 3D Artist and Photographer who has lived in The Netherlands for over 4 years, yet is still waiting to be granted official permission to remain. As a Stateless Palestinian born in Arab Emirates, he is currently in the process of seeking asylum.

I am Andrej Radman, a Croatian architect teaching architectural theory in the Netherlands.
For a long time, I have been introducing myself as a practitioner with a keen interest in theory.
Only recently have I concluded that this might not be accurate anymore. Practice is not opposed to theory. What comes first is action, both practical and theoretical. Moreover, action on action, before we reach the tangible. I look forward to the collective brainstorming on the topic of ground(ing).

Andrej Radman has been teaching design and theory courses at TU Delft Faculty of Architecture since 2004. A graduate of the Zagreb School of Architecture in Croatia, he is a licensed architect and recipient of the Croatian Architects Association Annual Award for Housing Architecture in 2002. Radman received his master's and doctoral degrees from TU Delft and joined Architecture Theory Group as assistant professor in 2008. He is an editor of the peer-reviewed journal for architecture theory Footprint. His research focuses on new-materialist ecologies and radical empiricism. Radman's latest publication is Ecologies of Architecture: Essays on Territorialisation (EUP, forthcoming).

I'm Theun Karelse from Borssele, which is a small village in Zeeland. The nuclear power plant is there. We speak a dialect, but this dialect can differ quite a lot. We in Zuid Beveland for instance speak very different from Zeeuw Vlaanderen, which lies on opposite shores of the Westerschelde.

Theun Karelse studied fine arts at the Sandberg Institute in Amsterdam before joining FoAM, a transdisciplinary laboratory at the interstices of art, science, nature, and everyday life. His interests and experimental practice explore edges between art, environment, technology, and archaeology. Lately he has been creating research programmes that consist of fieldwork and critical reflection. For this, diverse teams are established to address specific topics in specific locations by in-situ prototyping, experimentation, and direct perception.

Hi, my name is Sissel, I am a Danish artist living here in the Netherlands - in The Hague. In my artistic work I am interested in how we perceive, sense, and react to the (man-made) changes we experience in our surroundings. I often start from a place-specific situation where people experience environmental change, and zoom in on things that are less tangible, such as sensory experiences that hover on the threshold of what we can sense and understand.

Sissel Marie Tonn (1986, Copenhagen) is a Danish artist based in The Hague. In her practice she explores the complex ways humans perceive, act upon and are entangled with our environments. She is particularly fascinated by how our senses affect our ability to perceive change within an environment, affecting our capacity to act upon them. She documents and transfers certain lived experiences, where being amid a changing ecology might expose the psychological, social and perceptual/sensory challenges we all face in the present moment of volatile environmental change. She makes wearable, sculptural or performative 'props', that challenge and question the body's preconfigured modes of perception and attention and invites audiences to engage directly with them. These 'props' are meant to shed light on how our biology, as well as our cultural conditions — be it artifacts, forms of knowledge, or architecture - influence the ways in which we perceive and act upon our environments.

She completed a master in Artistic Research at the Royal Academy of Art in The Hague in 2015. In 2016 she was the recipient of the Theodora Niemeijer prize for emerging female artists and was a resident at the Jan van Eyck Academie in Maastricht in 2017. Together with Jonathan Reus and Flora Reznik she runs the initiative Platform for Thought in Motion, which hosts the Reading Room series.

Hello, my name is Flora Reznik. I am very excited to speak with all of you. I come from Argentina, where we speak Spanish with an Italian style. You'll notice that I always move my hands when I speak. I am an artist and together with an amazing group of people we've organized this event to ask ourselves what... hmm... the word in Spanish doesn't work. Ok, we will talk later.

Flora Reznik is a visual artist, researcher, curator, and videographer. She was born in Buenos Aires, Argentina where she obtained a Diploma in Philosophy (Universidad de Buenos Aires) and co-founded the Contemporary Arts magazine CIA, directed by Roberto Jacoby. Currently she is based in The Hague, The Netherlands, where she studied at the ArtScience Interfaculty of the Royal Academy of Art. Her work investigates issues of groundedness, territory and identity through a method of poetic abstraction. Her practice is shaped by artistic research: thorough theoretical research nourishes her artistic work. Her projects are non-medium bound and often incorporate video, text, and performance as well as sculpture and installation. She is currently busy with fictional narratives as a means to incorporate historical, philosophical and experience and field research. Questions revolve around belief and myth as an underlying force for what is considered "knowledge", in particular regards to the notions of progress, nature, and scientific certainties.

Collaboration and facilitating interdisciplinary learning and conversation compliment Reznik's practice. Together with Sissel Marie Tonn and Jonathan Reus, she co-organizes the ongoing project The Reading Room, a series of events engaging artists with scholars in a mutual exchange of knowledge, taking place at Page Not Found. She is the artistic director of Unknown Grounds, a performative symposium (2019) and publication involving interdisciplinary practitioners who gather to collectively explore the notion of ground and open community.

COLOPHON

Onomatopee 172
SCRIPT FOR A SYNTHETIC PLAY
On (Un)grounding community
and the generative power of fiction

ISBN: 978-94-93148-72-7

Editor and artistic director
Flora Reznik

Advisor
Agnes Winter

Author of 'Script for a synthetic play'
Nathaniel Feldmann

Authors of Collected texts
Andrej Radman
Bert Boekschoten
Bert Looper
Flora Reznik
masharu
Sissel Marie Tonn
Theun Karelse

Editorial advice and copyediting
Amy Gowen

Design
Studio Bramesfeld
bramesfeld.com

Print
Kopa, Lithuania

Paper
Cover: Crush olive 350g/m²
Inside: Holmen Trend 80g/m²

Typefaces
GT Haptic & Happy Times at the IKOB New Game Plus Edition

Publisher
Onomatopee Projects
www.onomatopee.net

Unknown Grounds I
Performative Symposium
took place in Leeuwarden, Nov 2019.
www.unknowngrounds.nl

This publication was made possible through the generous support of:

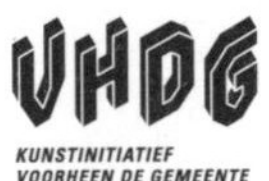

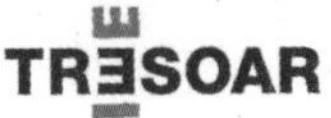

provinsje fryslân
provincie fryslân
Pauwhof Fonds
BankGiro Loterij

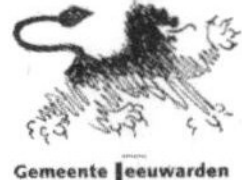

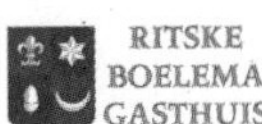

STICHTING HERBERT
DUINTJER FONDS